Finding Your Way to a Ph.D.
Advice from the
Dissertation Mentor
Second Edition

Lee M. Stadtlander, Ph.D.

DEDICATION

To the courageous and dedicated individuals who leave the path of their former lives to gain a doctorate..

CONTENTS

ACKNOWLEDGMENTS

My gratitude to the doctoral students who generously read and made comments and suggestions on early drafts of this book. They are, in alphabetical order: Quantrilla Ard, Yassi Ashdari, Meredith Baker-Rush, Emma Brooks, Brenna Doran, Judi Elster, Delores Hart, Marietta Miller, and Ethel Perry. In addition, my deepest thanks go to my friends and colleagues, Drs. Martha Giles and Daniel Salter for their suggestions and support.

CHAPTER 1
THE DISSERTATION

Congratulations on reaching the dissertation stage of your educational career! The path, you have chosen, to a Ph.D. is not an easy one. Ahead of you, there are both well-recognized obstacles (such as defenses) and ones hiding which will trip you if you do not have guidance. Any journey goes easier with a guidebook that explains the history of the locale, things you must see and things to avoid. This book is your guidebook to help you through the process of writing your dissertation. It will give you tips on handling committee members, writing various chapters, give you a refresher on statistics and qualitative analysis, and provide you with motivational messages along the way.

I am excited to be your mentor! Let me begin our journey together by introducing myself. I received my doctorate in Experimental Psychology from Ohio State University in 1993. I then was a professor at Montana State University (MSU) in Bozeman (I still live there). I worked at MSU for 11 years, then decided to re-specialize in Clinical Health Psychology through Fielding University (this is a second doctorate). I started working for an online institution, Walden University, in 2005 and am now the Coordinator of the Doctoral Health Psychology program. As part of this position, I give advice to students on the topics of their dissertations, working with committee members, etc. I found myself repeating the same information, so I started a blog (Ph.D. Realities: The Dissertation Mentor http://phdrealities.blogspot. com/), so students would have a place to see the answers to common problems and issues. This book grew out of the five years of blog posts.

A few words on the organization of the book, I try to walk you through the process of a dissertation in order, but there are a couple of quirks. First,

1

is while I recommend you begin writing your dissertation in Chapter 2, the literature review, I will discuss Chapter 1 first for clarity. Second, I want you to know there is a chapter of motivational thoughts (as well as, some motivational pieces in black text boxes in other chapters). When you are having a rough time, go there to get some extra support and inspiration.

I do not write this book in a formal style or format (although I will use the American Psychological Association's [APA, 2010] *Publication Manual* as the basis for formatting citations and references). I write to you, my mentee, directly and I will do so informally; my goal is to guide you step-by-step through the chaos and issues of completing your doctorate. Whether you attend a land based or online institution, you will find the issues I discuss to be relevant to you. All dissertation students must cope with writing, methodology, analytic issues, as well as, dealing with their dissertation committee. I assume you have had courses and training in research methods and analyses, and offer brief refreshers in these areas. If you find that you do understand research method terms or analyses I discuss, you should pick up a reference book in that area, to remind yourself of the issues. This book is written from a psychology perspective, so keep in mind other fields will have different expectations. So, my mentee, we will get started by considering: what is a dissertation and why is it structured the way it is?

What Is a Dissertation and Why Is It Required to Get a Ph.D.?

It might help to take a step back and consider, what is a Ph.D.? This is a Doctor of Philosophy; it is a research degree, meaning during the process of getting the degree you were trained as a researcher. Your dissertation is therefore the demonstration of your ability to conduct research and to write professionally. It is considered the terminal (or highest) degree in your professional field. Receiving the degree places you in an elite group (less than 4% of the United States population has a professional degree), and it is evidence of your professionalism and learning.

Why are you required to do research to show you are a professional? Conducting a research project shows your persistence and ability to complete a large project. It integrates all you have learned in your education and shows you can formulate new questions for future learning. Most degrees simply show learning; however, a Ph.D. also shows your ability to go further and explore unknown areas; to develop research, which answers new and unique questions. It shows you are a logical and critical thinker; you can synthesize ideas, data and information, and write in a technical and professional manner. Being able to conduct research also shows you are able to sift through information to find the current thinking in the field, as well as, able to apply theory to your thinking, practice, investigations, and current events. The dissertation is considered the first step in your future research plan for the rest of your professional life. Will you have to stay in this topic area? No, but you will have the ability to plan and execute future studies, no matter the content area.

At the completion of your project, you are assumed to be able to teach in your areas of expertise, both content and method, at a college or university level. No licensure beyond the doctorate is required to teach in post-secondary institutions.

Is the dissertation "just another paper to write?" No, it really is much more; it is a very formalized document which demonstrates your expertise in your chosen area of interest. Once you have completed the project, you are considered an expert in this area. The paper will eventually be published in dissertation databases, and will be a part of the professional literature. Other researchers and graduate students interested in your topic will read it in the future.

Students often feel there is too much emphasis on the formality of the dissertation. There are parts of the dissertation which do not make sense to them and as a result they do not give each part attention (a great example, is the abstract). First, it is important to understand your dissertation will be published, and much of the structure and formality is because of this. At one time, your final dissertation would actually be bound as a book and be in your university's library (you can still have it bound, if you wish). Of course, now everything is electronic, but the formatting remains as for a bound book. Possible formatting as a book is why the left margin is larger than normal (1.5"), to allow for binding.

There are a number of implications of these issues. (a) Your literature review must be correct and as complete as possible, both to demonstrate your expertise and also for future researchers. (b) Your research methods must be as accurate and complete as possible, so others know exactly what you did in your study. Consider the future researcher who does a study similar to yours but gets different results. He or she will want to be able to compare the two samples and methods to determine why the difference occurred. (c) Your paper must be written in the format required for publication, and the formatting will be checked before you receive your degree. (d) This paper will follow you forever. Any future employer or colleague will be able to look up this document. (e) For many students, your dissertation will be your first published work. Think of it as your first child: yes, you will make mistakes and when you look back at it years later, you will see things you should have done differently. For your future self, make it as elegant as possible and something of which you are and will be proud.

What Are You Going To Do With Your Doctorate?

It is important to consider your end goal before you get started! Many of the readers of this book are psychology students. What can you do with your doctorate in this area? First, it is important to understand in most states you cannot be licensed as a psychologist with a degree in an academic area (e.g., General or Experimental Psychology, Industrial/ Organizational Psychology and some Health Psychology programs). To be licensed, you would need to be in counseling or clinical psychology. So what can you do with an academic degree?

Many psychology students go into academia and work as instructors or professors, conducting research and teaching. What would your professional life be like as a professor? It depends a great deal, as to whether you have a full time or a part time position. Many beginning faculty members have one or more part time positions, particularly if they are working online. They may be teaching at multiple colleges or universities and teaching several courses at once. This means you would be online responding to discussions, grading papers, and interacting with students for many hours each day.

If you have a full time university position, whether online or in person, you would be expected to teach 2-3 classes a term, conduct research (or teach additional classes), and do committee work for the college/ university. If you do research, you will be expected to include students as research assistants, which means mentoring them in how to conduct research projects.

For a full time community/ junior college teaching position, you would probably teach 4-5 classes a term and participate in committee work for the college. You, typically, would not be expected to do research.

What can you do now to prepare for such positions? Get some teaching experience. With a master's degree you are qualified to teach at a junior or community college (no license is required). Another alternative is look at professional schools; as a grad student I taught an intro to psychology class at a paralegal school. The important thing is to get experience in front of a class. Save any teaching evaluations you get, this is proof of your ability as a teacher.

If you are interested in teaching at the university level, consider getting experience with research. If there are no research assistant positions available at your institution, consider applying for volunteer ones at local colleges or universities. You will get valuable experience, and may get the opportunity to be an author on posters or publications. Also, consider applying for a post-doctoral fellowship. These are (low-paying) paid positions after you have completed your Ph.D. and give you more advanced training in research. You will also have the opportunity to be listed on publications and presentations. The negative is it will take an additional year or two before you are in a stable faculty position. Plan ahead for what you want to be doing in your future.

The Key Players in Your Future

Let me introduce you to the key people involved in your dissertation. First is your dissertation chair (also may be called an advisor). This faculty member will work with you regularly on your dissertation. He or she is responsible for mentoring you through the experience. Expect advice from him or her in both research methodology, writing, the content of your paper, and the dissertation process. In some institutions, you may be in a dissertation classroom with your chair, in his or her lab, or work individually with your chair. He or she is responsible for monitoring the quality of your paper. Your chair is not an impartial reader: others at your institution will evaluate him or her as to your performance. Ideally, you can impress him or her with your writing skills, research knowledge, and persistence.

Next is your dissertation committee. Every institution has different rules on the number of faculty on the committee, however a few commonalities. Typically, you will need each person to approve your prospectus (or project idea), proposal (the first 3 chapters), proposal oral defense, final dissertation (all 5 chapters), and the final oral defense. These faculty members are resources for advice and assistance. More on these individuals and their roles are given in the chapter on committee members.

The Institutional Review Board (IRB). This committee, made up of faculty at your institution (and perhaps members outside the institution), reviews your project from an ethical viewpoint. They will be concerned as to whether you have clearly stated your research questions, maintained high ethical concern for your participants, and have clearly outlined your research method. Be sure to check your IRB's website for information on common ethical concerns. There will be more on these issues in the chapter on the IRB.

Where to Start?

You are ready to begin your dissertation… but where do you start?? First, you need a project idea, but how do you find one? Some students know very early in their program what they want to explore in their dissertation; however, if you do not know, here are some ideas as to how to come up with a topic. I suggest taking a couple of minutes and writing down what classes you liked, articles you have found interesting, and general topics which have interested you in your educational career. For the moment do not think about it in terms of doing a project; just consider things which have interested you. Let us say you came up with the following list:

Liked Women's Health class
Liked Changing Health Behavior class
Interested in pregnancy related topics
Interested in topic of cervical cancer
Found this article interesting:

> Manne, S.; Ostroff, J.; Fox, K.; Grana, G.; Winkel, G. (2009). Cognitive and social processes predicting partner psychological adaptation to early stage breast cancer. *British Journal of Health Psychology, 14*(1), 49-68.

Now just do some free association, here is mine: How about partner adaptation to cervical cancer? This makes me wonder if anyone has looked at partner adaptation to testicular cancer. I wonder if people have looked at cervical cancer and pregnancy. Is this an issue? What kinds of programs are there for partner support for health related issues? I wonder if I could do a program evaluation of one of them. Is there any secondary data (a data set that someone else has already collected) available on any of these topics (I should check out any institutional secondary data resources, which may be available)?

Ok, we now have a few directions to explore. Go to the library and do some searches on the various topics, include the word review in your search terms, only look at the last 5 years. This will bring up recent literature reviews on the topics. Read the articles paying particular attention when they talk about "future research" or "research needed". See if anything sounds interesting to you and follow it up with more articles, paying attention to the methods they use. I hope you will have at least a general direction by this point! Once you think you have found a gap in the literature, do searches to make sure no one has done the study you are considering. Write your search terms, databases used, and articles you found helpful in your research journal (more on this in the next chapter).

Too Close?

There is nothing like the panic a researcher feels when they find a study that appears similar to theirs! What do you do?? First, take a deep breath, rarely is a study going to be identical, so relax. I suggest your next step is to analyze the differences and similarities between yours and theirs (a spreadsheet works great for this).

Compare the population/ sample. How are they similar and different?

Look at their methodology. How are they different? What measures are used?

If you find they are similar, consider tweaking yours to add to the literature (this should always be your goal!). Perhaps adding a different variable or two would tell us more about the issue. If the previous study was quantitative, a qualitative or mixed methods study may provide interesting insights which are not evident in a quantitative study. Keep in mind that a major limitation of surveys is people are limited in their response to the choices given; they may have more to say.

Perhaps you can slightly modify your population to look at the issue in a new way. A hypothetical example might be originally, you wanted to look at diabetes in children and its effect on their schoolwork; your plan was to talk to the students and parents. Let us say you found a very similar study. You could tweak yours and look at the teachers' views of diabetic children in school. How knowledgeable are they about the illness and how do they see it affecting the children's work?

I often suggest students use the similar study as a contrast in their paper. Example: "Smith and Jones (2014) examined children and parents' views of the effect of the child's diabetes on schoolwork. The present study will extend this work by examining the perspective of the teachers of diabetic children."

How Long Should a Dissertation Take?

One of the most common questions I receive is "how long will it take me to do a dissertation?" Of course, my answer is it is very individual, it depends on how good of a writer you are, the type of study you do, and what problems you encounter.

Let us go a little deeper. Some students become convinced they should be done with their dissertation within the program stated requirement. However, this number has little to do with reality; it is simply the academic requirement. Dissertations do not go according to schedule; it will take however long it takes. Yes, I have seen students finish in one year, but I have also seen others take 2-3 years.

Why does it take so long?? There are a number of reasons. (a) Students may not write well, requiring many revisions and they must work with an editor. (b) There are many waiting times; each person who reviews your paper must be given a reasonable amount of time to complete it. Therefore, if you have to do many revisions, the time adds up. (c) Different research methods take different time periods. The fastest is doing an archival (a data set previously collected in the past) or secondary data (data collected by someone else, may be from an institution or organization) analysis. Probably qualitative and mixed methods take the longest. (d) Problems arise; in fact, expect them. You may not be able get the required number of participants, your computer crashes, you or family members get sick, or your boss insists you work overtime. Things happen, which delay the process. (e) Chair or committee issues: sometimes personalities clash, committee members get sick or even die. There is no way to predict such things and they too slow you down.

What are characteristics of students who are done quickly? They tend to be excellent writers, work every day on their paper, and the dissertation gods grant them minimal outside problems. Promise yourself today, however long it takes, you will keep working on it. That will get you done.

Learning

During the course of writing, collecting, and analyzing your data for your dissertation, you will learn a great deal. You will learn about technical writing, APA format, and more about your methodology. However, if you are observant and self-reflective, you can learn a great deal about yourself too. Occasionally take stock of how you approach this large task. Are you methodical and require a systematic plan be implemented? Are you a last minute person, trying to put something together before you have to meet with your chair? Think through the implications of your responses to these questions, how is your personality interacting with your desire to be done with your doctorate?

Do you need frequent feedback or are you a person who likes to work on your own and just get feedback when necessary? How do you handle criticism: do you become angry and defensive or do you look at criticism as a learning opportunity?

On what writing issues do your chair /committee frequently comment? Do you tend to get into the little details to such an extent your committee does not understand why you have included these issues? Common comments might be "please reduce the number of pages!" "Relate this back to your project." Perhaps you tend to follow interesting but irrelevant tangents in the literature, either never writing because you cannot escape the literature or writing about issues only tangentially related to your study. Consider, what leads you to these tendencies... how can you keep yourself on track?

How do you like to read articles, in print or on the computer? How do you (or do you??) organize these articles? Do you have piles everywhere or is your office very tidy? All of these clues are giving you information about yourself and your personality. Why not take a little time to think about how you are reflected in your work habits? These characteristics are not necessarily bad or wrong; however, it is an opportunity to decide if they are getting you where you want to go.

The Dissertation Process

Here is a quick overview of the dissertation process (be sure to check your own institution's exact process).

Prospectus. Typically, this is a short document, laying out your study ideas. Probably your chair and committee, and perhaps others must approve the prospectus.

Proposal. This consists of Chapter 1 (Introduction), Chapter 2 (Literature Review), and Chapter 3 (Research Methods and Analyses) of your dissertation. Typically, in psychology, these three chapters together are approximately 75-125 pages. Your chair will work with you on these three chapters. When your chair approves your proposal, it is sent to your committee member(s).

Oral defense of proposal. This is typically a 1-hour session with your chair and committee member(s). You will probably need to prepare a power point presentation of your study for your committee.

Institutional Review Board (ethics board, IRB). You will need to complete the IRB application (with all of the required materials) and receive their approval. You will also probably need to complete some type of ethics training.

Collect data using the steps approved by the IRB. If there are any changes to your methods, you need to get approval from the IRB. Your committee should approve any major changes in methods.

Analyze data, as you stated in Chapter 3. Your committee should approve any major changes in analysis.

Chapter 4 (Results) and Chapter 5 (Summary and Recommendations) are typically another 40-50 pages, with the full dissertation being all five chapters. When your chair approves your dissertation, it will be sent to your committee member(s).

Form & Style Review. The full dissertation is sent for the Form and Style review. Since the dissertation will be published, this review makes sure it is in correct publication format and the APA formatting is correct. (This step may be done post defense, in some institutions).

Oral defense of dissertation. This is typically a 1-hour session with your chair and committee member. You will probably need to prepare a power point presentation of your study for your committee.

DONE!

In the next chapter, we begin the dissertation process by getting things organized from your workspace to your computer.

CHAPTER 2
KEEPING ORGANIZED

One of the toughest parts of doing research is keeping track of the many pieces of information you collect. You not only want to find things the first time, but also be able to find them months later. You will want to be able to recall your rationale for making the decisions you made along the way and a timeline of when things were done.

First, think about your computer documents. A warning, I am a Windows person, so most of my software information is based on that. It is a really bad idea to just save everything into a single folder, like My Documents. I can guarantee before long you will not be able to find anything! Instead, create some folders within My Documents (more on this later in the chapter). I strongly advise saving every paper draft with the date it was written in the name of the file (do not overwrite your old file, save the draft as a new file). Yes, this means you will have a huge number of files eventually, but (and here is why it is important) if your chair comes back and says, "I think you should put back in the section you had on fish guts (or whatever)," you still have it and do not have to rewrite it. You also have a very nice record of the history of the project, and always know what draft is the most recent.

Always, always back up your files. Get an external hard drive, a flash (or thumb) drive, or a subscription to a cloud backup system and back up your dissertation files at least once a week. You can set your computer to back up automatically. Disasters occur. I have seen several students have their hard drive crash with no back up; losing whatever was on it.

I propose you need (at least) three separate organizing systems: (a) A research journal which keeps track of your day-to-day thoughts on your project. (b) Some way to keep track of references. (c) A future research

10

ideas journal where you can keep track of ideas for future studies. Now I will go into more depth on each of these.

The Research Journal

What will you write in your research journal? Everything you do on the project each day. To whom did you talk about the project, what did they say? What articles did you read, what are the important points from them? What ideas do you want to consider later? You can even get fancy and color code such things. You need to be able track the evolution of your thinking on the project and keep track of the day-to-day information, which will cross your desk/ computer/ mind.

There are many ways to approach this both high and low tech; the main thing is to be consistent with using it. You can certainly use a paper notebook and write things in it. Another alternative is to use Word or One Note. Again, more important is consistency of use. I have recently discovered some software I have been recommending: The Journal <davidrm.com/> (costs about $50). It is not the easiest software to set up, but is great once you do. It has a daily journal as well as what it calls notebooks, in which you can easily document your progress. You can set up multiple notebooks and diaries for different topics/ projects. You can also copy from other programs into it, allowing you to keep track of emails, citations, etc.

Here are a few recommendations from my Mac-user colleague, Dr. Daniel Salter. Evernote https://evernote.com is a cloud based note-taking and journaling software. It is also cross-platform, and plays well with other products, like Pocket. A Mac-specific product for notes, journaling, file management, etc. is DevonThink http://www.devontechnologies.com. It has a learning curve but can do pretty much everything a scholar would need, except generate a bibliography, as Endnote does.

References

The banes of every researcher's existence are reference articles. You have to have them and you have to find a way to organize them. I suggest you think carefully about how you like to read articles, in paper or electronic forms. Use that method when you set up your organization.

If you like to print out the articles, there are two common organizational methods. One is to have a file box (or cabinet) and file the articles in folders; it is often done by authors' names. A second method is to create reference 3-ring binders; these can be organized by topic, or author.

If you prefer to read electronically on the computer, I have some free software to suggest: Mendeley https://www.mendeley.com/ and Zotero https://www.zotero.org/ These programs were designed for researchers. They let you access all of your pdf files (a form of file that provides a copy of the original article, you typically use a program such as Adobe Reader to open them), organize them by topic, search the files, write comments, and highlight articles. They do not provide a way to write the reference in your paper. An option for references is bibliography software such as EndNote. I do not use this, because I am terrible about entering articles in the database. You will have to decide such things for yourself.

Future Research Ideas Journal

Unbelievably, someday you will probably want to do more research. If you go into academics as a professor, it will be required. So, make your future-self happy by writing down in one place research ideas, thoughts, and inspirations as you think of them. You will find that you will see interesting links between research areas as you read not only journal articles but also other books, movies, in conversations, etc. I use my journaling software for this, but any method will work, just be consistent.

Organizing Your Computer

An area students do not often consider is the organization of their computer files. Having a managed plan for your dissertation files will make your life much easier and you will be less likely to lose things along the way. How to you set it up? I suggest taking a few minutes and lay out on paper how you will want your dissertation folders and files to look; here is an example (if you are using a bibliography program, such as EndNote, it may affect your organizing scheme):

Dissertation
Data (SPSS files/ interviews, etc.)
Drafts
IRB
Literature
Resilience
Self-efficacy
Older adult
Research journal

Once you are happy with your plan, create a folder for Dissertation and subfolders for your other topics. Within your draft folder, keep every draft you create; do not just keep rewriting the same file. This way it is easy to go back and find the section you took out two drafts ago, and would be perfect now. Always have the date on each file and indicate, in some way, ones sent by and to your chair.

Using Referencing Software as an Organizing Tool

You can use referencing software such as Mendeley https://www.mendeley.com/, and Zotero https://www.zotero.org/ as a method to organize your literature. These programs have folders, which you can set up based on topics; you can then store your articles (in pdf format) within the folders. The software allows you to search the articles, make comments, and highlight. The articles are also stored online, which lets you access them through other computers, in a sense creating a portable library.

The Research Journal as an Organizer

I previously mentioned setting up a research journal. This is a journal, either on your computer or on paper, where you keep track of everything related to your research project. If you have it on your computer in Word or OneNote, I suggest using a Research Journal folder and separate files within it. Therefore, it might look like this:

Research Journal
Dissertation progress notes
Library
Future research ideas

This will make it much easier to find things later. Within each journal section, I suggest always including the date and you may find it helpful to post the newest item at the top of the page. That way you do not have to scroll down to find the end.

If you use a paper version, consider using some type of dividers; you can use post it notes as dividers for this if actual folders are not practical. Divide your journal similarly to the sub files above and always date your entries.

In the section, "Dissertation progress notes" keep a running log of what you are doing on your dissertation. It is also a good idea to write down comments from your chair or committee member. This is where you can vent your frustrations and share your excitement.

In the section on "Library" write down your search terms and databases used. You might want also to keep track of articles you want to look up or ones people suggest to you.

In the section, "Future research ideas" keep track of the connections you see to other possible research studies. Even if right now, you do not see yourself doing research in the future, write them down anyway. Someday you may be in a position to conduct more research and this will give you a start (or suggestions for future students).

Organizing Your Workspace

One of the most difficult parts of conducting research is not the method or statistics; it is keeping track of all of the articles, books, information, data, and ideas, which accumulate during the process. For most people desks, tables, and the floor may become covered with files, print outs, and small scraps of paper. Things can easily become lost or misplaced and you lose track of where you are. What can be done?

I think you need to consider seriously your own personality: are you willing to invest time and effort to set things up and maintain it? It is the maintenance, which often gets lost... so think about that. What are your current work habits? Do you have a dedicated space, like an office, or are you transient in your work? Organization will only work as far as it fits with your work habits and personality.

There are many approaches to this topic, over the next few sections I will make some suggestions you might want to consider regarding your workspace. Always, think about your own work habits, it is better to make gradual changes you will keep up then to make drastic changes and not maintain them. The point is not to make you feel guilty; it is to get you organized!

The Transient Workspace

What are the signs you have a transient workspace? You are a transient when you do not have an office or space, which is yours alone. When you find yourself having to pack up all of your papers, computer, etc., so the family can have dinner or if you tend to work out of a tote bag most of the time, you fit this profile. It is difficult to keep things organized when you are transient, but I have a few ideas for you. You need a file cabinet to keep your work together and help you organize. Think creatively as where to put it; it can find its home in a closet, under the stairs, or in the laundry room. The main point is to have a place where you organize articles and keep your papers in one space.

You also may want to consider a tote bag, basket, or box where you keep your materials, which you are currently working on. Keep your pens, paper clips, calculator, and any other small items you may need in a small box or bag so you can find them easily. Consider having some brightly colored folders that you can use as a color coding system (e.g., red folder has articles on self-efficacy).

When you are at the data collection/ analysis stage keeping organized becomes even more important for the transient. If you have paper copies of data and or consent forms, you must keep them confidential and secure. I suggest using manila envelopes to categorize them and having a locked file cabinet or other locked space where you keep them. Yes, it seems like over kill in some ways, but for the transient you must make a special effort to protect the confidentiality of your participants. As you do not have your own space, you are using public areas to which anyone entering your home has access. Make the effort, and have some locked spaces; there are small lockable filing boxes available, which would be quite adequate.

Shared Workspace

Now, I want to consider people who have shared workspaces. You fit this category if you have your own workspace and it is in a shared part of the house. Therefore, if you work at a desk in the family room, kitchen, bedroom, etc., you fit this category.

The shared workspace has some advantages over the transient one, work does not have to be moved frequently and there is stability in your work process. However, it does share with the transient space the lack of privacy. You may have to work with the TV going in the background and other people coming in and out of the room. This becomes of concern when you reach the data collection phase. As with the transient, you need a locked file cabinet, somewhere you know that no one else has access. Think about the worst-case scenario, your child decides to use a completed survey to draw on or to cut it up for a craft project for class. This is a breach of confidentiality and it is required you report it to the IRB.

If you use a desk, it does allow for piling of information, which can quickly get out of control. To help with this tendency you may want to get a plastic organizer with vertical or horizontal dividers. I suggest setting one day a week for filing paper, that way it does not get out of control.

The Dedicated Office

What do I mean by a "dedicated office"? It is a room used primarily as an office; it may temporarily be used for other functions, such as a guest room, but it returns to its office use. The advantages of an office are having a door you can shut (and perhaps lock), reducing the noise and intrusions. Of course, if you have children, a door may not make much difference! In general, it makes it easier to maintain privacy and confidentiality of your data. I still, however, recommend a locked cabinet, to reduce any chance of a breach of confidentiality issue (the IRB will insist upon it). The disadvantages to having an office in a separate room are you may feel cut off from your family and you may need to enter transient mode when guests take over the room. As a transient, make sure you remove or lock up any papers or data you are working on. Otherwise, you may discover the guest has accidently packed them and taken them home. I want to make it clear the workspaces I have discussed are not "bad," they each have challenges; such challenges are just a part of working from home, which must be dealt with.

What do you need to include in your office? A desk or table, large enough to spread out papers is essential. A lap top or desktop computer, monitor, and a printer are must haves. Optional equipment, but nice to have is a 2nd monitor (allows having several documents/ programs open at the same time) and an iPad or tablet for travel. Beyond those key pieces of equipment, a good lamp, a file cabinet, and bookcases will make your life more organized. Consider having an organizational system with your books, arranging them by topic helps, and some people arrange them within topic by author. Books you use frequently, keep close to your desk (for me, they are some statistics books and the APA manual). I also have on my desk: a calculator, some small note pads, pens, and sticky notes. I also have a white board in my office for reminders and tracking projects. In the next chapter we will begin thinking about your project and writing.

CHAPTER 3
WRITING

By definition, writing is a task done alone, with minimal distractions. Such an environment can be difficult to find in a busy household, particularly with small children. You will need to find a way to deal with these needs. Some suggestions from other students: find a space, which allows you to close the door, even a large closet will work. Recruit or hire a babysitter for a couple of hours to allow you some writing time. Work early in the morning, late at night, or during your lunch hour.

One way, to structure your time, is to set goals for yourself for each week of the term, leading to a final goal for the term. Hold yourself to these goals. You can even break it down further and set a goal for each day. Consider if you wrote just one page per day, in a 11 week term you would have written 77 pages! Some people set an alarm; they must sit and work on the paper for an hour, until the alarm goes off. The important thing is to develop some work habits, making your dissertation a priority. If you do not have time to actually sit and write, read journal articles, write in your journal, or share progress with a friend. Even a baby step is a step forward. Otherwise, it is just too easy to let the rest of your life take precedence. Your paper is not going to shout at you to write it. Your chair will probably not nag you. You have to make the decision that receiving your degree is important enough to set time aside every day to work on it.

Isolation

Do you feel like you are all on your own working on your dissertation? Feelings of isolation are very common with everyone working on a dissertation (both online and in person in a traditional brick and mortar university). Here are some things you can do reduce the feelings of isolation:

 • Have a dissertation buddy. This is typically someone else working on his or her dissertation who agrees to be a support person with you (as you will be for him or her). Set up regular times to make contact, and make a commitment for a specific length of time you will work together (maybe a term to start).

 • Have a dissertation mentor/coach. This is often someone who already has his or her Ph.D. (although it does not have be) and agrees to be your support through your dissertation process. Keep in mind their experience may be different from yours, so watch for advice, that may not be applicable. This person is for support and you need to feel accountable to them.

 • Have a dissertation support group. This is a group of students who are working on their dissertation at the same time; it may be an in person group or virtual (e.g., a texting) group. Have the group set up some specific guidelines, for examples, you will all email/text each other at least 3 times per week. Share both your dissertation experience and personal issues that arise for the most benefit.

 • Have monthly meetings with your dissertation class. If your chair cannot (or will not) set this up, do one in google hangouts. Talk about where each of you are in the process and problems you are encountering. Problem solve and find solutions!

To get the most out of these support systems, tell them what you are working on this week and what you want to accomplish for the next week, set realistic short-term goals. Be accountable to them and expect accountability from others. Live up to your promises for contact, they need you as much as you need them.

The Pain of Writing

Writing is painful. Sorry, that tends to be everyone's reality. It is hard work to think through complex ideas and find the best way to present them so someone else can understand them. A few general things, first if you find it very hard to write, I recommend this book:

Saltzman, J. (1993). *If You Can Talk, You Can Write*. Grand Central Publishing.

As you can see, it is an older book, so it is available very cheaply at online bookstores. It will reduce your anxiety and will help you get something down on paper. I strongly recommend reading your paper aloud; you will catch many errors. If nothing else, read to your dog or cat, they will find you fascinating! You will reduce the number of needed corrections by simply rereading your paper carefully. It is often helpful to set it aside for a few days, and then read it with fresh eyes.

Be prepared and open to many revisions. Your committee has much more experience in writing at this level, trust their guidance. At a doctoral level, revisions are simply part of the writing process. Professionals also have to rewrite their papers many times; keep in mind that the final article you see in the journal has little resemblance to where it started. As an example, a recent article I published with colleagues went through 25 revisions (yes, I counted!).

What should you look for in revisions? Read a sentence aloud and see if you can restate it more clearly. You want to be very precise in your meaning. Let me give you an example from one of my papers I wrote with some colleagues. Here is the original draft of the first few sentences of the paper:

By 2020, one in six American citizens will be elderly or over 65 years old (U.S. Census, 1993). The number of oldest old individuals over 85 years old will reach 6.6 million in 2020 and is expected to triple by 2050 and reach 18-19 million (Administration on Aging [AoA], 2010). The rapid growth of the elderly and the oldest-old population is a growing concern to the healthcare system, as it must prepare to provide increased support services.

The 2000 U.S. Census (2001) reported 4.2 million people were over the age of 85 (1.5% of the population), this group has been designated the "the oldest-old" by demographers, and is the most rapidly growing age group. Currently the cost of health service utilization for the oldest-old averages $22,000 per year compared to $9,000 for individuals 65-74 years old (Krause, 2010).

What is different? The second version is much clearer, concise, and more to the point than the first version. The focus was changed from future issues to present ones using statistics to bolster the argument concerning costs.

It is important you understand the dissertation from the faculty's viewpoint; it may explain much of their writing-related feedback to you. Throughout the dissertation process, and even after its publication, your committee's names are attached to your dissertation. When anyone at your institution criticizes a student's dissertation work, one of the first questions asked is "who is the chair?" The student is expected to make errors; it is the chair's role to catch as many as possible.

Finding Articles

I suggest starting to write your dissertation with Chapter 2, the literature review. How do you start? How do you do library searches and not be overwhelmed with distantly related articles? The first step is doing the outline of your Chapter 2, including your variables (I will talk more about this shortly, also see the example outline of Chapter 2 in Appendix D). Then you are ready to begin the library search. Pick a variable and get started!

If you are in psychology, you may want to start your search in the psychology databases; however, be sure you check related ones too (e.g., Thoreau, Sage, CINAHL, Medline, ERIC). Start with getting some general background on your topic. Say you are interested in "resilience" in older adults, begin with a search of resilience, review, and older adults (you will also need to try elderly and aging). This search will bring up literature reviews on the topic. Let us say there are three reviews, which look to fit your interests. Read those. These articles will have references, which relate to your specific interests, look those up. In addition, take note of the keywords lists with each of your articles; they may offer suggestions you had not considered.

When you find mention of theories, make a note of authors related to the theories. Look up those authors, you may find additional information on your topic. Keep in mind you are expected to understand the history of the theories. It is very important you are keeping a research journal as you search. You need to keep track of your search terms and databases used, as these will be included in Chapter 2. You should also keep notes as you go, perhaps marking articles, which you want to be sure to read carefully.

Alternative Sources for Articles

Students frequently ask me how to find articles that are not available in the library. Here are a few alternative sources. Make sure you have checked Google Scholar, also check electronic professional media such as LinkedIn or Research Gate. These are sites where authors frequently post preprints (work not yet published) as well as published articles. Be sure you have checked all of the available databases in your library. In psychology, one that is frequently missed is "Psychology: A SAGE Full-Text Collection."

This database has many psychology articles, which for some reason, are typically not picked up by PsycINFO. If you are interested in a health related topic, make sure you check CINAHL (a nursing database) and Medline.

See if your library has "Thoreau: Search Multiple Databases." This often pulls up articles not found in individual databases. Similarly, the database, "Academic Search Complete" brings up some information outside the regular databases.

If you still cannot find a particular paper you are looking for and if you know the authors and title, you can request an interlibrary loan, in which the librarian will track it down for you. As a dissertation student, you may be allowed only a certain number of free loans, so check the rules out first.

Those are the easy sources there are some other alternatives. If you have a college or university near you, you might check if they have the article you need. If all else fails, you can write to the author, although this will probably require some detective work. You can try the email he or she listed in the article (often listed on the abstract page), however, be aware faculty tend to move around a lot, and it may no longer work. The problem is you usually do not receive any notice the person no longer works there, so if you do not get a reply you do not know if they are just rude or never got it. If you know what affiliation (college, university, etc.) they listed on the article (it is usually listed near the title or as a footnote), go to the institution's website, and see if they are still employed there. They usually provide email addresses. If you still cannot find the author, do a Google search on him or her; you may pick up a clue where they work now and can try to track down an email address.

What do you say when you write them? Tell them you are very interested in their work on X and ask if they could send you a copy of their article (give the citation for it). Also, ask them if they have any other papers in this area. Be sure to include your mailing address in case they want to send it that way. Here is a sample letter:

Dear Dr. Jones,

I am very interested in your work on fear of pencils. I am a doctoral student in psychology at XXXX University and my dissertation is in this area. I have been unable to locate your paper Jones and Smith (2010) "Fear and Pencils: How do I function now?" I would greatly appreciate it if you could send me a copy of this article. In addition, if you have any subsequent papers in this area, I would love to get copies of those too.

Thank you so much for any help you can provide,

Suzy Student
17 Hopeful Lane
Johnston, NY 98765

Unfortunately, some people are rude, and you may not get a response. Give the author a week or two to respond; the final step would be to try to track down other authors on the paper.

Theory and Research Design

One of the common issues students have when they are beginning to think about doing research is how all of the pieces, which are necessary, fit together. Do you begin with the research design and try to find a study to fit it? What is the deal with theories, where do they fit into the thinking? There actually is a way to clarify these pieces. Let us begin even broader by considering reviewing the literature. What does that mean? It means finding recent articles on your general topic of interest and beginning to read. Notice what theories the authors discuss when talking about the topic. After you have read 10 articles or so on the topic, stop and evaluate. Are there consistent issues mentioned? What theories were discussed; did the authors make predictions for their study based on the theory? If you are not seeing any predictions or discussions about how the theory is impacted by the new findings, you need to look for a new theory. It is important that you are able to make predictions based on the theory you will finally use.

As an example, say you have narrowed the search down to two theories. It is time to go back to the library and find some review articles using those theories. When you have read those, you should have good understanding of the theories and how they relate to your topic of interest. Think about the variables other researchers have used, which are related to your topic and how the theory suggests the variables should interact.

Putting Theories to Work

As an example in order to think things through, I will be using the patient-by-treatment-context interactive model of Christensen and Johnson (2002). The model proposes that the relationship between patient characteristics (e.g., personality and beliefs) and patient adherence (e.g., preventative care) is moderated by the treatment context (e.g., primary health provider characteristics and behavior). I like to draw things out so I get a better understanding of it.

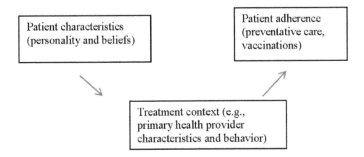

We can begin tweaking some of the variables and think about how they would be affected in the model. For example, we could consider patients who do not have faith in modern medicine and the issue of vaccination use. The model suggests it is the primary health provider (PHP) who is the determining factor, so if the PHP was understanding of the patient's beliefs, according to the model, it should increase vaccination use. This is how we went about this process so far:

Literature review $\longrightarrow$ Theory $\longrightarrow$ Predictions

Theory and Research Questions

Previously, we considered theories and that they should lead to predictions. Now we take it to the next step and use those predictions to develop research questions. We examined the patient-by-treatment-context interactive model of Christensen and Johnson (2002), and we predicted it is the primary health provider (PHP) who is the determining factor, so if the PHP is understanding of a patient's nontraditional medical beliefs, it should increase vaccination use. Now we can develop a research question based on the prediction.

RQ1: What is the relationship between PHP's support of patients' nontraditional medical beliefs and patients' use of vaccinations?

To use this research question we would need to have a way to measure "PHP's support of patients' nontraditional medical beliefs" and also a way to measure the patients' beliefs. If you are able to find such measurement tools in the literature, great! You could do a quantitative study measuring PHPs' support, patients' beliefs, and the actual use of vaccinations. However, let us say you could not find such measurement tools. You have a couple of choices: 1) develop your own measures or 2) do a qualitative study to examine the opinions of both patients and PHPs. This last choice would require two new research questions.

RQ2: What are PHPs' opinions about patients' nontraditional medical beliefs and vaccinations?

RQ3: What are patients', with nontraditional medical beliefs, opinions about their PHPs and vaccinations?

Here is how we went about this process:

Literature review ⟶ Theory ⟶ Predictions
Research Questions ⟶ Research Method

Notice, I did not start with the method, rather I let the theory, predictions, and research questions determine the appropriate research method to use.

Integrating Research as You Write

Students frequently ask me, what is the best way to integrate research as I write? This is one of those issues everyone has their own way of doing. I will share mine, keep in mind I am already familiar with the field; you will need to read extensively before beginning. I tend to read sections of articles then go to my document and summarize what I read and add a citation. Here is an example, an original article:

Professionals involved in the training of psychology graduate students, both in educational and clinical settings (e.g., practicum and internship), need to understand the role of stress among students to provide guidance on effective stress management and self-care (Myers, Sweeney, Popick, Wesley, Bordfeld, & Fingerhut, 2012, p. 55).

I would paraphrase it as: It is important that psychology faculty involved in graduate student training understand and be able to offer student assistance in stress related self-care (Myers et al., 2012).

Some things to notice, I did not say something like "Myers et al. (2012) stated that...." These types of phrasings read very choppy and come across as unprofessional (I always think of it as undergrad-like). You want your writing to flow and tell a story, it is not a simple listing of study after study. If you find yourself writing lists of studies, it is time to stop and rethink what you want to say. What point are you trying to make about the studies? Think about it on a higher level than the individual studies, what is linking those studies together, what is the overarching theme? Then write about the higher-level issues bringing in the individual studies as examples.

Avoid quotes as much as possible; only bring them in if they add something unique to your argument. Check out peer-reviewed articles; you will find quotes are very rarely used.

Reviewing Your Own Work
The Micro Level Review

How do you review your own writing? Why should you spend time on this? Doing a good review of your writing before you send it to your chair or other committee member can save you a great deal of time in the end. Remember, every time a faculty member reads your paper they are allowed a reasonable time to review it, if you can reduce the number of reviews needed, it can save you months!

I recommend a several stage process of self-review; you can do the steps in any order that feels comfortable for you. Yes, it will take you time and it is not particularly fun, but it will save valuable time and it will teach you to write! First, review your writing at the micro level of individual paragraphs and sections. Make sure you have spell check and grammar check turned on in your paper. If you are not seeing some words/ sentences underlined in red or green in Word, go to the options menu (often listed under File)/ proofing and make sure spell and grammar check are turned on. Make sure the Exception boxes are not checked (these turn off spelling and grammar checks). Make sure that you then check all of the items in red (spelling) and green (grammar issues) underlining.

Step 1 is to pick a small section of your paper; read the section aloud, carefully listening for grammatical errors and missing words. You may also wish to consider utilizing and submitting your work, or even small sections of your work to electronic/online academic writing aids such as Grammarly and/or Turnitin. Check with you school as they may already provide students with access to these or other writing tools and aids.

Step 2, read through the section again checking for APA errors. There are several common problems students have, for example, citations and use of the second person ("we," "our"). Read those sections of the APA manual and make sure you are doing them correctly. Make sure any jargon is defined (a good rule of thumb, would your grandmother or friend not in your field, understand the term? If not, define it).

Step 3 is the hardest one, check your content. Make sure you are only talking about one topic in each paragraph. Are your arguments clear? Does every fact or statement have a citation? Check the length of your paragraphs and break up long ones (there should be no page long paragraphs).

The Macro Level Review

We now move to a macro level in which you make sure the chapters and the paper as a whole are consistent. As you write over time, it is easy for your paper to deviate in your methodology and approach. If you have ever read a new novelist's first book, you may have experienced the situation in which the details in how they describe a character or scene changes throughout the book ("Mary" may change from being "an auburn haired beauty" to a woman named "Marie, with golden hair" by the end). This is a lack of good editing. The next stage of your self-review should be as an editor.

To do this, you need to read the entire paper in one sitting. You need to keep track of any inconsistencies or changes in methodology descriptions; I like using track changes' comments for this, but you can also use your journal for note taking. Do not change things during the reading just note the problem areas. It is important that you are able to read the paper without interruptions, because you want to be able to remember details. Things to check carefully include the description of theories throughout the paper, are you always using the same terms? Check your research questions and hypotheses; are they the same in Chapter 1 and in Chapter 3? Are your descriptions of your methodology the same in Chapter 1 and Chapter 3? Are the topics introduced in Chapter 1 discussed in Chapter 2?

When you review the full five chapters of your final dissertation, it is even more important to double-check the details. Are Chapters 1, 3, 4, and 5 all consistent? Did you do the methods and analyses in Chapter 4 you discussed in Chapters 1 and 3? If not, explain why they changed. Read Chapter 1 and then read Chapter 5 make sure everything is consistent; particularly look at theory issues. Make sure you have discussed all of your results in Chapter 5 you mention in Chapter 4. Each of your key findings need to be discussed in terms of the literature and the implications in Chapter 5. Compare the headers listed in the Table of Contents with your document to make sure they are all accurate.

A final check is to print out your references, then go through the paper and cross off each reference as it is cited. They should come out even. Make sure citations with 3-6 authors list all the authors the first time cited, and then use et al. When it doubt, check the APA manual for the correct citation. Make sure you have a DOI (Digital Object Identifier), for each article. These are 10-digit numbers unique to each article. They can be found on the first page of electronic articles, near the copyright notice. They are also listed in library databases for each article. Keep in mind some articles, particularly medical ones do not have a DOI.

All of these self-reviews will take you some time, but you truly will save yourself a great deal of waiting time in the end. In addition, you will be a much better writer for doing it. Eventually, you will do these reviews as you go and it will take much less time.

Common Writing Problems

Personal Pronouns. English (as with many languages) has three levels of personal pronouns:

	Singular	Plural
First Person	I, me, mine	we, us, our
Second Person	you, your	you, your(s)
Third Person	he, she, it, him, her, it, his, her(s), its	they, them, their, theirs

APA does not allow the use of first person plural "we" or "our" (the exception is if there are multiple authors). The broader use of the word "we" (often referred to as the "editorial we" or "royal we") leaves the reader wondering to whom you are referring. Instead, substitute an appropriate noun or clarify to whom you are referring. Here are some examples for a dissertation.

Incorrect: We know the elderly …
Correct: Researchers have found the elderly ...
Incorrect: Drug use is common in our country
Correct: Drug use is common in the United States.
Incorrect: We will contact possible participants by …
Correct: I will contact possible participants by…

Avoid Absolutes

In the social sciences, unlike the hard sciences, there are few absolutes. What do I mean by absolutes? We rarely know facts about humans that we are confident will never change or have no possible exceptions. Here is an example: While many elderly people are less active than when they were younger, you can probably think of exceptions of people who are actually more active. Therefore, the statement "The elderly become less active with age" would be an incorrect absolute. A better statement would be "The elderly tend to become less active with age." This allows for possible exceptions and avoids the perception that it is a rule for everyone.

This issue becomes even more important in Chapter 5, when you interpret your results. Avoid over-generalization, for example "the findings clearly show elderly feel …" You have only examined a sample of the population, you have no way of knowing if everyone in your population would feel the same way. Restrict your interpretations to your sample, point out differences between your target population and your sample's characteristics. Here is an example from a recent paper (Stadtlander et al., 2013):

It is important to consider the generalizability of the current study. This study examined relatively healthy, independently living, oldest old adults recruited through online students' social networks; thus, the results are specific to this group and may not be generalizable to the general population of oldest old. This sample is only generalizable to the extent other individuals share the sample's key demographics.

When to Summarize, Paraphrase, and Quote

In the social sciences, we rarely quote, so you should typically be emphasizing paraphrasing and summarizing. Summarize when you are giving the gist of a study or theory. Paraphrase when you want to represent a source more clearly or pointedly. Paraphrasing does not mean changing a word or two, you must replace most of the words and phrasing with your own.

Only use quotes (exact copy of material) when:

- The quote is evidence that backs up your reasoning. An example might be if you are making the case that child abuse has profound psychological effects: a quote from a reliable source giving specific statistics would support your statement.
- The words are strikingly original or express your ideas so compellingly that the quote can frame the rest of your discussion.
- They state a view you disagree with, and to be fair you want to state the view exactly. Be sure you include page numbers and quote the passage exactly as written.

What is Alignment?

Alignment is one of those tricky issues you know when you see it. It is getting at the idea that the research questions, hypotheses, methods, analysis, as well as the literature all align or are consistent with each other. An example of nonalignment might be bringing in new variables in your research questions that were not mentioned previously in your paper. Another example is saying you are using grounded theory (which relates to qualitative studies) in your quantitative study. It seems obvious when I say it, but the problem is you are writing the paper over time, and sometimes things drift away from the original plan as you discover new literature and have new ideas.

Here is where the outlines come in handy, laying out your plan in an explicit way helps to keep everything aligned. Going back and frequently reviewing your research questions and hypotheses helps. Keeping a research journal makes a big difference! Have near the front of the journal or add a sticky note as a marker to the page with your research questions and hypotheses, so you can reread them frequently.

There is no easy way to make sure everything is aligned, you will have to check and recheck as you write. Have a sticky note on your monitor: "Is everything still aligned and consistent?" Make sure when you are writing about your research method, the language is correct for the method. Faculty members often see qualitative studies talking about correlations, there are no correlations in qualitative research! This is not aligned. Before you start working on descriptions of your research method, pull out a book on your method, and refresh yourself on how things are worded and phrased. Make sure all variables and topics in your study have been discussed in your literature review, problem statements, and purpose statements.

Conciseness

One of the hallmarks of professional writing is that it is clear, organized, and concise. I recently reviewed a final dissertation 450 pages long; it is painful to wade through that much information. The reality is if you are writing that much, you are probably repeating yourself and not being concise.

How do you make your writing concise? First, make an outline of each chapter and stick to it! There is a tendency for people to be attracted to distantly related articles, and start to go in strange directions. An outline will keep you focused on the essentials. When you think you are done with the chapter, go back to the original outline and make sure you have not taken any wandering paths. There may be times, as you are writing, that you realize or discover that including an additional subsection[s] in your chapter may make your discussion more poignant or clear. Make sure to revise and update your outline to include any additional sections you have added to any chapter.

Second, never copy a section from a previous chapter into a later one. I know it is more work to actually rewrite a similar section, but trust me; your reader will appreciate not reading the same paragraphs repeatedly. Besides, you may make new interesting connections or have flashes of inspiration when you rethink the section. You will also have a tendency to write more concisely the second (and third) time.

Third, make sure you have grammar and spell check turned on in Word. Pay attention to the grammar and writing marks shown in Word (those green and red lines that appear under words and sentences). Right click your mouse on them and they will offer suggestions, follow them.

Fourth and this is the tough one, reread each sentence and think about how you could write it clearer. Eliminate adverbs (e.g., "mostly," "almost"), eliminate extra "thats" (my own problem area). Put the paper aside for a day or so, then go through it again carefully and make sure each sentence works with the previous one and is clear.

Finally, pay attention to the total number of pages. Think about whether you would want to read that much. Please do not send your committee a paper with 450 pages! In the next chapter, I will discuss how to get along with and interact with your committee members.

CHAPTER 4
COMMITTEE MEMBERS

I like to have my students contact their committee member(s) once a term, just to update them on the student's progress. Typically, the committee member does not need to be involved in the process until the chair approves the proposal (first 3 chapters of the dissertation). However, if you have questions on methodology or content you should ask them.

They will review your proposal and give you feedback on it, they are another set of eyes, and will see the paper fresh; after all, your chair has read it many times and may no longer see problems. Committee members will review your proposal and be at your defense.

If the committee member is your methods expert, you may wish to contact them as you complete your Chapter 3, Institutional Review Board (IRB, ethics board) application and begin to collect and analyze your data. I encourage you to use them as a resource. You may want to run Chapters 4-5 by them, for their input. They will review your final paper. They will also be at your final defense.

The Care and Feeding of Committee Members

What is appropriate behavior for a dissertation student toward his or her chair and committee member? In a traditional brick and mortar program, you may see behaviors modeled by students further along in your program, but it is difficult at an online school to know what is normal.

The reality is at both online and brick and mortar schools it varies tremendously, so the first bit of advice I have for you is to ask what your chair and committee member prefer. If your chair does not suggest it, ask for a phone call to get you started, and discuss what their expectations are of students. What are they expecting from you in the first term? How will they decide if you should get an "Unsatisfactory" or a "Satisfactory" in the dissertation course? How would they prefer you to address them?

In advance, think about how you like to work; are you independent and good at personal goal setting? Then perhaps ask if you could send them your draft once a month (or whatever the two of you agree is appropriate). Are you a person who has a hard time structuring your time and goal setting? Then ask for help as to what is realistic. You might want to set up regular meetings or times when you will need to submit drafts. Talk to your chair about your needs, and how they can be accommodated.

Also, ask your committee member when they would like to see a draft. Many will prefer you wait until your chair has approved the proposal, unless you have specific methodological or content issues on which you want their advice.

A few general bits of guidance, be polite, ask questions when you need help, no one expects you to know everything. A "thank you" for good advice, prompt response, etc. means a lot to faculty (think of it as positive reinforcement, they will tend to repeat the good behavior).

This is important: No one will know you are having problems, unless you say something! Typically, if they do not hear from you, the faculty's assumption is you simply do not care or are not working on the paper. Many people can help if you run into problems. Consider hiring an editor to work with you (check with your university/ department/ program, they may be able to recommend some editors). If one of your committee members advises you to get an editor, then listen and try not to be defensive. They are trying to save you time and tuition money! If you have committee issues, contact an administrator in your program/ department. Be assertive, it is your money and time being spent, however, always be professional in interactions with faculty and administrators. Emotional responses are never a viable solution.

Faculty are people too, with busy schedules and family obligations, it is not realistic to expect immediate feedback. However, if you have not heard from a faculty member at all within a couple of days of contacting him or her, write an email and double check. Ask if they can give you an estimate of when you might get a response. Again, be polite and professional.

Remember, every faculty member who reads your paper is allowed time to respond. I know it is hard to wait, but go on to the next stage. If you are waiting to get feedback on your prospectus, then go ahead and start on Chapter 2. If you are waiting on your proposal approval, work on your IRB application and power point for your defense. There is always something to work on. If you cannot find anything else, do an update in the literature and see if anything new has been published, which could be helpful.

What do you do if you are having problems with your chair? First, write out an email outlining the issues, say how you would like it to be resolved, be very professional, no emotional response. Often it helps to take on some of the responsibility. It is a good idea to let it set for a day to make sure you are not being impulsive. Here is an example of an appropriate email:

Dr. X,

I am concerned it is often taking 3 weeks for you to review my proposal drafts; the delay is really slowing my progress on the paper. Is there anything I can do to make this process go a little faster? If it would help, I could just send you a couple of pages at a time. Ideally, I would like to be able to get a response on my writing within a few days to a week. Do you have any further ideas?

If you feel you do not get a satisfactory response, the next step would be to contact their supervisor and ask for help. One final bit of advice, keep a record of when you submit papers to faculty, when you get a response, and their comments. Such a record may be needed in the future (this is where a research journal comes in handy!).

Make Things Easy For Your Committee

What is your ultimate goal of being in a doctoral program? It is to be done and have that diploma! One way to speed the process along is to make it as easy for your committee as possible. What do I mean by making it easy? When you send drafts to your committee, leave their former track changes in place and use track changes as you write. This way they only need to check the changes you have made. Does it make you crazy to see the track changes? It is possible to turn on track changes, so it is keeping track of what you have altered, but not show it as you write. In Word 2010 go to Review/ turn on track changes/ under final show markup, choose "Final". It will not show the changes as you type but it is saving them. Then when you are done, choose "Final: Show Markup" and they are shown (if you have a different version of Word, check the help menu). If it feels wrong to send a track changes document, you can also send a clean draft with all track changes removed. However, do send both versions.

How else can you make it easy for your committee? Make sure you address each comment from the faculty member. You may disagree and that is okay, but indicate why you disagree in a track changes comment. It needs to be more than a simple "no, I don't want to change this." You need a good rationale.

Other ideas: write to your committee member once a term (assuming you have not talked to them recently), and give them an update on your progress. Sometimes I do not hear from a student for years, and do not know if they dropped out, are on a leave of absence, or just slow in their progress. Do not forget to thank them occasionally for their help everyone likes to be appreciated!

When Should Your Chair Review Your Paper?

This is a tougher question than it appears, chairs may have specific policies as to when they want to review drafts. I have heard a range of ideas from end of chapters, weekly, monthly, to a full proposal. Personally, I like to see a draft every couple of weeks at a minimum, for a couple of reasons. (a) I know the student is working. (b) The student is less likely to end up having to rewrite massive amounts if I am keeping them to the expectations.

I have offered an accelerated option to my students, which you may want to run by your chair if you are interested. Students can lay out their term goals by the week with a "deliverable" (writing assignment) due every week. The idea behind this is to keep them working toward a deadline and getting more accomplished. If you are a person who works best on a definite deadline, you might want to consider such an option.

What do you do if your chair wants fewer reviews than you feel you need? I suggest asking for a phone call and discuss your needs with him or her. Have a definite timetable for reviews in mind. Discuss why you feel a more frequent review would help you (e.g., make sure you are on track, you are a person who needs more established deadlines, etc.). What if he or she refuses this request? You could hire a private editor (make sure they know your institution's style and expectations). The important thing is you do all you can to move yourself along the process.

Accepting Feedback Gracefully

An inevitable part of working on your dissertation is getting criticism. This can be very difficult for some students; they feel defensive and resentful. Please, take a step back from this and think about it, a faculty member has taken a great deal of time to read and review your paper. They do not like saying negative things any more than you like to receive them. However, it is the faculty's job to help you learn to write, and that is what they are doing when they give you feedback. It does not matter if a hundred other people think you are a marvelous writer, accept this person does not, and see how you can fix it.

How should you approach the feedback? I suggest quickly reading the feedback and if you find you are feeling defensive close it and think about it for a while, resist the impulse to immediately write back. Remind yourself they are trying to help you learn to write professionally, and they want you to be done. Then when you feel you are ready (hopefully no more than a day!), begin the revisions, take each comment one at a time, think about it and revise. If you find you are not sure what the faculty means with a comment. Carefully write out an email of inquiry. Here is an example:

> Dr. X,
> Thank you so much for your thoughtful comments and suggestions! I find I do have a question about comment LX5, in which you state: "I don't know what you mean here." Could you clarify please, do you mean the sentence itself is not clear or do you mean the word "finaglosity" is not clear in this context?
> Thank you again for your help,
> Jane Student

Always be polite, and thank them for their help. You will find you get much further with being open and kind than you ever will with being defensive.

Chair Talks

I often suggest you talk to your chair about problems and issues, but what is the best way to do it? I have a few suggestions for you. Write down questions and topics you want to cover in your talk, this way you are sure to get the answers you need. If you need to discuss something that makes you uncomfortable, it is often a good idea to write out what you want to say, this way you are sure of your language and know you are saying exactly what you want. It also may help to practice speaking with a friend or spouse about difficult topics.

Be diplomatic. You want to have a long-term relationship with this person, do not lose your temper, and say something you will regret later. If you feel you are losing your temper, say you need to go and will speak with him or her later. Always be polite, being aggressive really does not help your case, it simply puts your chair on the defensive. Remember, faculty members are also constrained by many rules, your chair cannot speed up the process for you, nor can he or she skip any steps. Your chair is simply your guide through the dissertation process.

I suggest always making an appointment to talk to your chair, even if they have specific office hours, that way you know he or she will have time just for you. Give him or her an idea of how long you will need to talk. 5 min? Half an hour? You want them to have the time available for you. If you want to talk about a specific part of your paper, highlight it, and send it in advance via email.

It is often helpful to approach the call as a way to learn and improve, as opposed to telling the chair how you want to do it. Trust your chair knows the way through the dissertation wilderness and will guide you, if you take off on your own; you risk wasting a great deal of time and having to backtrack.

How to Complain

As an administrator in a doctoral program, I commonly receive emails from students complaining about something: their chair, committee member, IRB, etc. I think it important for you to consider how such emails are received; ones written in a calm, clear, and professional voice are much more likely to be taken seriously than when someone rambles for pages, is demanding, and threatening. This may seem somewhat counterintuitive; is not the threatening one more serious and angry? Perhaps, but the author also comes across as someone who does not understand the system and is not looking for solutions, they simply want to vent.

How can you be taken seriously when you are upset? I suggest first opening Word and just dump all of your emotions and frustrations into the document; lay out everything that happened and how you felt about it. Feel better? Okay, delete it and start fresh.

Start a new document, now unemotionally lay out the sequence of events that has led to the current issue. Include the dates; do not personalize or say how you felt about it, just give the facts. Once you have a clear timeline, write a brief summary of the history, again no emotion.

Now I want you to think about what you would like the reader to do about the issue. How do you want them to help you? Would you like him or her to suggest some solutions? Would you like him or her to speak to your chair and possibly mediate? Add that in as a polite request.

It is time to write the final email. First, introduce yourself to the email recipient, where are you in your program? What program? Have you ever met him or her? State you are seeking their help/ advice/ etc. with a problem with (whomever).

Copy the brief summary into the email. Then add the section on what you would like the reader to do for you. You may add one sentence with how you are feeling about the problem (e.g., "I am feeling very frustrated, and would deeply appreciate your input"). End the email by thanking them for their help. If you have emails or documents, which show the history or in some way support your claims, attach them. I suggest you then let the email set for a day, read it again when you are calm. If it sounds clear and professional, go ahead and send it. In the next chapter, your study officially begins through developing a prospectus.

CHAPTER 5
PROSPECTUS

The prospectus is the first official document related to your dissertation (your institution may have a different name for this preliminary summary of your study idea). The prospectus will be a summary of your project; it is usually a fairly short document. In it, you explore a summary of the literature (clearly showing there is a gap in the literature) and flesh out your research method. It is important to remember you are building a case in your writing; you want to clearly show there is a need for your study (answering the "so what?" question, which is your gap in the literature). Then, you want to show clearly how your study will fill this gap. Make sure everything in your paper is aligned: your literature, research questions, hypotheses, and method all address the same issues and are consistent. Your analyses should be consistent with your hypotheses and research questions.

You will want to consider the long-range implications of your study, do not overstate this, you will not change the world. You are adding a little more to the literature, hopefully, clarifying your small piece of the puzzle. Check out what guidebooks are available through your institution on the prospectus. These can guide you in your writing.

If you are planning to use a vulnerable population (e.g., your subordinates, children, elderly, prisoners, people who are ill, etc.) or if you are thinking about having people participate in some sort of activity or program (e.g., a new relaxation technique; something they would not normally do) then you may have ethical issues to consider. First, go to your IRB's (Institution Review Board /ethics board) website, there may be information available on these issues. Think the issues through and talk them over with your chair. It is probably a good idea to write up your method and the issues with your vulnerable population in an email to the

IRB, and ask for their opinion and if they foresee any problems. Most IRBs are open to this early planning and it can save you much pain and disappointment later.

Often, by the time you are writing your prospectus you have a chair of your committee, and you will be in close contact with him or her. Beware of the tendency to think of your dissertation as MINE. It is not your paper, it is a paper written by you at the advice of your committee. You will be asked to write many revisions. No, it does not mean you are a bad writer; you are learning to write in a very technical manner, which requires precise clarity. Your committee member(s) (and particularly your chair) are there to guide you and get you and your paper through the many obstacles ahead. Patience, persistence, and meticulousness will save you a great deal of pain in the future!

Once your chair has approved your prospectus draft, it will be sent to your committee member(s). He or she will probably want revisions. You may be required to get additional approvals on it.

Starting To Write

You are staring at a blank white screen; you write your name down… now what? Starting to write a dissertation feels very scary. However, let us take it a little bit at a time. For now, all you want to do is an outline of your prospectus. That is workable. So pull out the requirements for the prospectus, and copy down the topic headings they give you (they will probably be similar to this):

Title Page
Problem Statement
Significance
Background
Framework
Research Question(s)
Nature of the Study
Possible Types and Sources of Information or Data
References

Hey, you already have half page! You can do this! I suggest starting with the background section, this is the literature review. Start with an outline of what you feel needs to be discussed, this will keep you from wandering off into other tangents. Let us say your topic is partner adaptation to testicular cancer. Your main topics will be:

Testicular cancer (always start with the broadest topic)
Partner Adaptation

Now think about some subtopics. Under testicular cancer, you would want statistics (look at the National Institute of Health and American Cancer Society [ACS]). Next, you want to include the effect of the cancer on the patient and family (check ACS). Under partner adaptation, you should talk about other research on partners with other forms of cancer. Then discuss any research that has looked at testicular cancer and partners. End with a statement indicating the gap in the literature and how your study addresses the gap. Always pay attention to the research methods used in previous studies. Therefore, our final outline is:

I. Testicular cancer
    A. Statistics (look at National Institute of Health and American Cancer Society [ACS]).
    B. Effect of the cancer on the patient and family (check ACS). Research methods?
II. Partner Adaptation
    A. Research on partners with other forms of cancer. Research methods?
    B. Testicular cancer and partners. Research methods?
    C. Statement of gap in the literature and how study will address it.

To help you get you started, I have included a sample prospectus outline in Appendix B and a draft of a sample prospectus in Appendix C.

Prospectus: Problem Statement and Purpose

The first page of your prospectus is your cover page. Center the word Prospectus, under this and give your title. Your title should be no more than 12 words (per APA) and should include the topic, the variables and relationship between them, and the most critical keywords. Also on the cover page, include your name, any other required information, double-spaced and centered under the title.

The next page begins with your problem statement. It should include a logical argument showing an identified gap in the research literature, which has relevance to the discipline and area of practice. You should briefly review the literature in this section and demonstrate this is a true gap. Provide three to five key recent citations that highlight the relevance and currency of the problem.

Next, describe the overall purpose or intention of your study. In quantitative studies, state what needs to be studied by describing two or more factors (variables) and a conjectured relationship among them related to the identified gap or problem. In qualitative studies, describe the need for increased understanding about the issue to be studied, based on the identified gap or problem. In mixed-methods studies, with both quantitative and qualitative aspects, clarify how the two approaches will be used together to inform the study.

When your reader finishes this section, he or she should understand why you are doing the study, and the gap your study will address. Have someone unfamiliar with the topic area read the section and see if he or she understands it. Spell check and grammar check!

Prospectus: Significance

The significance section of the prospectus informs the reader how your study will contribute to your discipline. Sometimes it helps to realize you are "selling" your study, convince the reader it is necessary. Describe how this study will contribute to filling the gap you identified in the problem statement. What original contribution will this study make? Keep in mind this is the main criterion that will be used to determine whether your study is of "dissertation quality." Discuss how your research will support professional practice or allow practical application. This part should answer the "so what?" question. Picture your chair asking you: "So what? Why do we need this study?" Keep in mind you are defending your choices through facts (not opinion) and should provide citations. Build a case as to the need for your study.

Finally, discuss how the significance you have highlighted aligns with your problem statement to reflect the potential relevance of this study to society. This is getting at the bigger picture: How might the potential findings lead to positive social implications? Use the "4Ds" as you think about the implications: death, disabilities, disease, and dollars.

Prospectus: Background

In the prospectus background section, it is common to have literally a list of relevant studies. However, keep in mind if you choose to do it this way, it must include information as to how each article relates to your study. You need to provide a representative list of scholarship and findings that support the main assertions in the problem statement, highlighting their relationship to the topic (e.g., "The variable XX was studied with a similar sample by Smith (2010) and Johnson (2008)," or "Jones's (2011) examination of industry leaders showed similar trends in the same key segments").

Think of this section as a way to demonstrate you have done your homework on the topic and are demonstrating it to the reader. Make sure you include references you have cited earlier in the paper and how they relate to your study. When the reader finishes this section they should feel convinced you have done a good preliminary literature check and have identified the most relevant research for your study.

Prospectus: Framework

This section of the prospectus is examining the theory you will be using in your study (this is not the qualitative method you will be using). Describe the theory(s), then take it to the next step and lay out what the theory predicts will happen in your study. If you find you cannot come up with predictions, it may not be an appropriate theory. To develop predictions, think through each step of your study and how it relates to your theory. It may make it clearer to give you an example from a recent article I wrote with some colleagues (Stadtlander et al., 2013):

The patient-by-treatment-context interactive model of Christensen and Johnson (2002) provides the framework for the study. The model proposes that the relationship between patient characteristics (e.g., personality and beliefs) and patient adherence (e.g., preventative care) is moderated by the treatment context (e.g., primary health provider characteristics and behavior). The model has been successfully applied to specific illnesses; for example, renal insufficiency and hemodialysis (Christensen, Moran, & Ehlers, 1999) and cardiac rehabilitation (Christensen et al., 1999). It does not appear to have been previously applied in the present context of ongoing preventative care in older adults. The patient (Locus of Control [LOC], resilience, self-efficacy, beliefs, and behavior) and treatment (Primary Health Provider [PHP] characteristics, health behaviors) variables in the current study were derived from the literature and are consistent with this model.

From the perspective of the patient-by-treatment-context interactive model of Christensen and Johnson (2002), adherence (preventative care) is expected to be best when the patient's characteristics (personality and beliefs) are consistent with the treatment context (PHP characteristics and behavior; Christensen, 2004). Thus, in the current study, there should be consistent preventative care (adherence) when the patient has higher internal LOC (being proactive in health), higher resilience (inner strength and optimism, health-promoting behaviors) and higher self-efficacy (more likely to seek information and self-confidence) and to indicate that they like or feel comfortable with their PHP (treatment). In addition, it would be expected that there would be less preventative care (lack of adherence) when the patient has lower internal LOC (i.e., external; not proactive in health), higher powerful others and chance scores (increased trust in PHP). Other expectations include lower resilience (higher level of subjective complaints, fewer health-promoting activities), and lower self-efficacy (less likely to apply health interventions [preventative care] and less self-confidence) and to indicate that they do not like or feel comfortable with their PHP (treatment).

Prospectus: Research Questions

The next section of the prospectus is your research questions. The research questions are your overall questions/ issues you are examining in your project. Keep in mind research questions are NOT interview questions (a common error), they are the more overarching questions. For a quantitative study, you should indicate any survey measures you will be using in your study in the research questions. Let me give you as an example, some research questions from the Stadtlander et al. (2013) mixed method paper. There were three primary research questions for the study:

(RQ1 qualitative) How do the oldest describe their relationship with their primary health provider relative to their reported health practices?

(RQ2 mixed methods) How do scores on the personality measures self-efficacy (as measured by Schwarzer & Jerusalem's, 1995 measure), resiliency (as measured by Wagnild & Young, 1993 measure) interact with primary health provider relationship descriptions and reported health practices?

(RQ3 quantitative) Schwarzer and Jerusalem (1995) and Halisch and Geppert (2012) reported self-efficacy correlates with LOC in younger elderly individuals. Does this relationship continue into the oldest-old age group?

Prospectus: Nature of the Study

In the section Nature of the Study, you should describe your study methodology. The reader of this section is expecting to see specifics of how you will conduct your study. If you are using surveys, which one(s) will you use? How many participants are you planning to have? How did you arrive at this number? How will you recruit your participants? The more information you can provide, the better the reader can see you understand the research methods you are proposing to use.

Prospectus: Possible Types and Sources of Information or Data

The section is asking specifically, in your study what data will you use? Some possibilities include: test scores from college students, employee surveys, observations of children, interviews with practitioners, historical documents from state records, de-identified medical records, or information from a federal database.

Inappropriate sources to include in this section are literature you are reading, your committee, and any other data you have not previously addressed in the prospectus. This section should merely be a summary of what you have previously discussed in terms of data.

Finally, state how you plan to analyze your data. If you are doing a quantitative study, indicate the statistical tests you are planning and the dependent, independent, and moderating variables. Will you need post-hoc tests for your analyses? Indicate if post-hoc tests are appropriate (if you do not remember what these are, check out the chapter in this book on quantitative analyses).

If you are doing a qualitative study, how will you analyze the data? Be specific about coding and themes. If you are doing a mixed method study, indicate how you will examine the quantitative and qualitative aspects separately and together.

Prospectus: Overview.

You have written a first draft of your prospectus, congratulations! However, there are still some things to work on. Make sure all parts of your prospectus are consistent, make sure you are using appropriate terminology (e.g., do not use terms like "correlation" when talking about a qualitative study). In quantitative studies, make sure the research questions align with methods/ variables, and your analyses.

Prospectus: Faculty Review

You have finished a draft of your prospectus and sent it to me as your committee member, what am I looking for? I typically read through the paper twice. The first time I am looking at APA formatting, spelling and grammar issues. Be sure you double-check your citations and references with the APA manual; I will look at those closely. If you use any acronyms or abbreviations, make sure you spell them out the first you use them. If you use jargon (e.g., self-efficacy, locus of control, resiliency), make sure you define it (even if you think I know what you mean). A good rule of thumb is: would someone not familiar with your field of study know the term? If not, define it.

I then read it again concentrating on content. I want to make sure you are consistent in how you are describing your study throughout the paper. For example, if you are doing a qualitative study, you should not be using terms like "correlation." I will make sure your research questions are consistent with the literature you reviewed and your theory makes sense for your study. I will look for some predictions with your theory, as to how you expect the study to come out. I will look for evidence you understand your analyses and they make sense given your research questions. By the time I finish your paper, I should feel confident you understand the topic area and you are capable of doing the study. Finally, I will print out your references and go through the paper crossing off references as they are cited. They should come out even, no extra references or citations.

Personally, I use track changes and make many comments. I try to be clear in my concerns, but would always want you to ask for clarifications if you were not sure what I meant. It is better not to guess if you are doing things right, save yourself some time and ask about issues.

Rewriting

You have rewritten your prospectus umpteen times for your chair. It is sent to your committee member who wants more changes. What is all this rewriting about? Are you really that bad of a writer?

Rewriting is an integral part of professional writing (as is criticism). It is tough to go back through and rework it again and again. However, it truly is part of the process and prepares you for peer review of future articles you will write. You are writing a very technical paper and it is easy to make errors, and not be precise. Keep in mind that changing things in one section of the paper often means having to change other sections. Always read the entire paper before resubmitting it, and make sure everything is consistent. There are no quick fixes in rewriting, but I can make a few suggestions.

Be gracious in accepting feedback; do not argue with the reviewer. If you truly feel he or she is wrong on a point, make an argument in a comment in your paper (support it with literature, APA manual). Always be polite, thank them for taking the time to read and critique your paper.

Carefully go through each comment and change it as needed. If it is a grammar or formatting issue, check the entire paper and make sure it does not show up again. Yes, I know how time consuming it is, but it will save you time in the end. While you may want to use the Replace function in Word, make yourself check each suggested change before replacing it. English is a fickle language; often what is correct in one circumstance is not in others, so double check.

Try reading your paper aloud to catch problems. If you find this does not work for you, ask someone who is a good writer to proof it for you. Again, no arguing! Thank them for helping you.

It is a great idea to keep notes of common problems you have in writing. You can then double-check these issues before submitting it to your reviewers. Read your writing critically, have you made clear arguments? Have you supported each statement with citations?

I find it helpful to think of rewriting as a challenge, I want to outwit the reviewer by making it as clear and correct as possible. While rewriting is not particularly fun, it can be a learning experience and will make you a stronger professional.

Never "Done"

I am often sent drafts from students saying they are "done" with a section. It is so important to understand that you are not done with any part of the paper until the university approves the final draft. Every time a faculty member reads a chapter or section, he or she is sure to spot something they missed on previous reads. Why does this happen? Every time it is read, the reader is in a different cognitive mode. They may have recently run into issues with other students on APA format or grammar, and will be more aware of the issue when they read your paper. They may be more awake than previously or just had a cup of coffee.

Why is this important for you to remember? Because if you are in a mindset that you are done with a part of the paper you will tend to not reread it and add in new thoughts or ideas. It also makes you resentful and defensive when a reader points out problems, which is never good. You are writing a book; therefore, you must keep checking everything is consistent and written correctly. You would be very annoyed with a mystery writer who changes details between Chapter 1 and the middle or end of the book. It is similar with your dissertation, it is a whole project; while it is written in parts, you must continue to think of it as whole. The goal is to have the best dissertation you can have, to reach this goal, graciously accept criticism, make the changes, and learn about writing as you do so. In the next chapter, I give you some motivational thoughts to use when you need them.

CHAPTER 6
MOTIVATIONAL THOUGHTS

As you begin writing your proposal, you will inevitably have times of doubt, when you feel like you need some extra support from your mentor. This chapter is for those times. If all is going well feel free to skip ahead to the next chapter. When you need some support, come back to this chapter and picture the two of us sitting together with some coffee or tea as I help you get back on track.

"A-Motivation"

A-motivation, paralysis. A time during a project when you cannot take that next step, sitting down at the computer seems impossible. Whether your paralysis is due to a fear of failure, lack of belief in yourself, learned helplessness or a lack of belief in the value of what you are trying to achieve, it feels hopeless. How to get out of this slump??

A few suggestions. First, I strongly suggest that you get yourself a support group; it is very hard to complete a dissertation alone. How do you do that? If you know anyone locally working on a dissertation, you could have an in-person group. You could ask people in your dissertation class or others you know at your institution to join with you in a virtual group. I have had a text support group for students in my dissertation class; you could form one too. Everyone in the group agrees to text when they think or work on the paper and to also offer support and encouragement to the group. Does a group seem too much? Then get a dissertation buddy, one other person who will agree to support you (and you will support them) at least once a week by email, text, or phone.

Second, put together an "Achievement File". Sometimes we need to remind ourselves, that we are bright and capable. The Achievement file is for this. Include the successes you have had; those papers that you got an A on, maybe your transcript showing your great grades, the ribbon you won at the state fair, and the photo of your kids, anything that makes you proud of your achievements. When you feel down, pull it out, and remind yourself, you have done great things before and you can do it again!

Third, perhaps it is time to tweak your project. Consider, what would make you excited about the topic again? Are you tired of thinking about children and eating disorders? Maybe moving it to adulthood would give you a fresh perspective and enthusiasm. Maybe switching from eating disorders to another topic would help. Sometimes just switching chapters helps, a shift from literature to research methods may be all you need.

If you have tried these and other ideas, and you still cannot get interested, perhaps you need a break. You can take a leave of absence for a term, get your head together, and come back refreshed. If you go this route, I suggest really taking a break from school; read those trashy novels in your closet, go to the beach or mountains, do something very different from your regular life. Give yourself a chance to recharge and think about the bigger issues of life. What do you really want to be doing in 5-10 years? What do you love doing? What makes you excited to get up in the morning? Where does getting a doctorate fit in the picture?

Fear

Where does fear fit into your dissertation journey? Is it in the front seat, screaming at you at every turn? Is it driving? I have been reading Elizabeth Gilbert's (author of *Eat, Pray, Love*) new book, *Big Magic: Creative Living Beyond Fear*. She has a wonderful letter she writes to fear that I would like to share with you.

Dearest Fear: Creativity and I are about to go on a road trip together. I acknowledge that you believe you have an important job to do in my life, and that you take your job seriously. Apparently your job is to induce complete panic whenever I am about to do anything interesting and, may I say, you are superb at your job. So by all means, keep doing your job, if you feel you must. But I will also be doing my job on this road trip, which is to work hard and stay focused. And Creativity will be doing its job, which is to remain stimulating and inspiring. There's plenty of room in this vehicle for all of us, so make yourself at home, but understand this: Creativity and I are the only ones who will be making any decisions along the way. I recognize and respect that you are part of this family, and so I will never exclude you from our activities, but still - your suggestions will never be followed. You're allowed to have a seat, and you're allowed to have a voice, but you are not allowed to have a vote. You're not allowed to touch the road maps; you're not allowed to suggest the tours; you're not allowed to fiddle with the temperature. Dude, you're not even allowed to touch the radio. But above all else, my dear old familiar friend, you are absolutely forbidden to drive.

I love this imagery! While you need fear to keep you motivated on your dissertation journey, you do not have to let it be in charge! Over the next few posts, I will be sharing more insights from Gilbert's book.

Creativity and the Dissertation

Is working on a dissertation a creative process? I believe that it is, yet not in the way of the creativity of writing fiction. In fictional writing, you are creating a new world, one that may or may not reflect reality. A fiction writer has rules that must be followed in form and must, in a sense, build and support the world that the story is set in. However, the end point is created by the author; when starting the book or story, the reader does not know exactly where the story will go.

In writing the technical material of a dissertation, you are constrained by the specific rules and formatting. However, you must develop an idea and project that has never been considered before, something new and therefore creative. You must support your creative idea with literature and it should build on previous work, but it is your own creativity that moves the project forward. The reader of your dissertation also does not know where your "story" will go, that is an outcome that is determined by your data.

Catching Creativity

I have been discussing Gilbert's (2015) book on creativity. She talks about the ebb and flow of creativity as something you seem to "catch" as it flies by, almost as if it is alive. The key point that she makes is the need to be working daily so the writer is in a position to be available when the creativity "arrives." She discusses the need for the writer to work on his or her craft daily, recognizing there will be days when the creativity is available and the words flow without effort while other days one must work hard for every word.

This relates directly to your dissertation, in that it is important to work on it in some way every day. If you wait until creativity happens, your wait may be long and little work be done. Recognize that your creativity will ebb and flow with days of great insight and days when you struggle to write a sentence. The important element is to be there every day, working on your dissertation, so you are in ready to catch creativity when it makes an appearance!

A Trick for Inspiration

Gilbert (2015) discusses a trick for inspiration: stop complaining. Every time you express a complaint about how hard it is to be creative or write your dissertation, inspiration takes a step away from you, offended. "It is almost like inspiration puts up its hands and says, 'Hey sorry, buddy! I didn't realize my presence was such a drag. I'll take my business elsewhere'" (p. 118).

Instead of complaining how difficult it is to write a dissertation; face the real reasons you decided to get a doctorate. Put aside the rationales that you may give to others and face the fact that you probably chose to go into this field because you love it (and if you don't, you should not be doing it!). So try saying, "I love my creativity and my dissertation."

By saying that you love your work, you will draw inspiration to you. "Inspiration will overhear your pleasure, and it will send ideas to your door as a reward for your enthusiasm and your loyalty" (p. 119).

Pain and the Dissertation

Gilbert (2015) discussed writing blocks and the pain that often both causes it and results from it. As I considered this related to writing the dissertation, I realized that there is an issue with psychology dissertations. In psychology, it is common for students to take on a topic that is related to their own experience, let's use as example, domestic violence. The student may have been in a violent relationship in the past, and wants to examine some aspect further in her study. However, such a close association with a topic can cause emotional pain to the extent it becomes almost a posttraumatic flashback. She may find herself reliving the experience as she reads other people's accounts and at the data collection phase, personally hearing others' experiences can be very traumatic.

I commonly advise students to avoid such emotional topics, as they often result in pain at the thought of working on the paper, and cause their own version of a writing block. A student may be more comfortable with a related, but less personal topic, such as the experience of working in a domestic violence shelter. Do not set yourself up to have an emotional punch in the stomach every time you work on your dissertation. It will not be long before you choose to avoid the pain.

Student Realizations

What realizations have you gained since starting your dissertation? Here are few things other students have reported.

"Writing a dissertation is harder than I thought it would be." This is a common realization that students have, they went into the process, having written many papers before; however, writing a dissertation is very different. It takes longer to research the literature, write, conduct the study, and revise than most people assume it will take. There are also many approvals you will need along the way; each person will want more changes.

"I was surprised that I actually enjoyed the process." I hope students discover this one. Writing the dissertation is an intellectual challenge, it will force you to grow, to stretch, and to develop as a professional. Most researchers have a deep intellectual curiosity that research satisfies. It allows you to ask interesting questions and to find out the answers. Enjoy the process!

"It is a much more lonely process than I anticipated." For online doctoral students, this is a very real aspect. You need to develop a way to counter this. Get a support group, find a dissertation buddy; you need someone to talk to that is also going through the process.

"My family is supportive, but they just don't get the work involved." People who have not gone through it, do not really understand how difficult the process is. It may help to share with them the day-to-day highs and lows, and incorporate them into the process. Help them to understand both the pressure and your drive and motivation to succeed.

"My defense was much more collaborative that I thought it would be." I often hear this comment. Students expect that a "defense" will be confrontational, but it rarely is. It tends to be colleagues working together to come up with the best possible project.

"I was surprised that I ended up really sick of my topic." Unfortunately, this is common. Many people become quite burnt out on the dissertation topic and do not want to do anything further on it.

"Writing a dissertation changed me." Often, I hear this at graduation. Going through the dissertation process makes you a better writer, able to cope with constructive feedback, become more compulsive in your research, and provides a deeper appreciation of your topic and participants. We often talk about social change, but also realize that you will be changed by going through the process.

Faculty Realizations

Previously, we looked at student realizations of the dissertation process. Now we will look at realizations of the process from the faculty point of view.

"I am surprised at how easy it is to get a journal article out of the dissertation, and how few do it." Very few students take the extra time and effort to publish the data from their dissertation. Yes, it will take some time to put it together, but you have already done all of the hard work! Talk to your chair or committee member about helping you write an article (and offer them second authorship on it).

"Students do not understand what a chair is supposed to do." Students are often confused about the role of a chair. He or she is not an editor and is not a co-author. They are more of a mentor, guiding you in the direction that you need to go to get done. Many faculty will offer editorial and writing advice, but it is not required.

"I am shocked at how much time students waste." Students often procrastinate with the dissertation, it feels overwhelming and they are not sure how to get it going. You probably had specific times set aside when you worked on coursework; it helps to do so when writing too. If you feel stuck, get help!

"Students ignore feedback from faculty." Many times students resent advice from faculty, and choose to ignore it. This leads to more delays in getting done. Typically, faculty have been through the process before and know what is required. If you ignore their advice, you are wasting their time and yours.

"Many students do not read all of the documents provided and other completed dissertations." Other people have solved the problems you are having right now in your writing and in the dissertation process. Take the time to read all of the documents available, and save yourself time and money!

Facing the Monster under the Bed

As you lay awake at night, what are your dissertation fears? That you are not good enough? That you will run out of money? That you will not get your Ph.D., your family will be ashamed of you, and you will end up on the streets? Just as when you are were a child, these are the monsters under your bed.

First, rest assured that such fears and worries are very normal. Often the best way to handle the monster under the bed is to directly confront the fear. You are worried that you are not good enough? Let us examine that. How did you do in your undergraduate and graduate programs? You got As and Bs? Then you should be able to handle the dissertation. Think about (it helps to actually list them) your successes academically, what were you really good at? What always was a problem for you?

What do you feel is your weakest area related to your dissertation? Do not just worry about it, take control of the monster! Is it writing? Then look into taking a writing course. Look into hiring an editor to work with you.

Is your weakest area research methodology? Then read some books in your methodology area, so you feel more confident.

Beware of the common tendency to close your eyes and pretend the monster is not there, while you quiver in fear. Face it and wrestle it to the ground! You are in control of your destiny, take whatever steps you need in order to get rid of the fear and get done!

Criticism

How do you deal with criticism? A few common examples are: being told that your writing needs help, that you have to do yet another revision, or that you are not going to be done this term, because the paper needs more work. There are a number of possible responses to such news. You can deny that there is a problem; you can argue with the critic; or you can pout and refuse to respond to them.

A better solution is to take control and ask yourself: what can I do to fix this? If writing help is suggested, listen to the comments. Form a plan of action. It may help to talk to the faculty member and talk through the issues that he or she is seeing in your paper.

Criticism is always difficult, no one likes to be told bad news, and faculty do not like to give such news. However, both parties must keep the end goal in sight: to get you done. Think of it as doing whatever it takes. If it means working with an editor or rewriting that chapter one more time, do it. You do not need to feel embarrassed, it is not a failing of yours; it is simply one more step that must be taken on this long journey.

Remember that you go into the dissertation process with an academic idea of what to do in order to complete a research project. The final dissertation is an applied proof of your research ability. Of course, you will not be great at everything! That is why you have faculty available to consult with you. It is why only experienced researchers are faculty mentors, this is a difficult process, and everyone has problems along the way.

Be tough, listen to the criticism, and move on. Learn what you need to learn; after all someday you may also be a research mentor!

Be a Puppy!

I recently adopted an 8-week-old keeshond puppy, Mandy. Several things have struck me about the puppy personality: enthusiasm, curiosity, and engagement. I think these are key issues for you and your dissertation as well!

Puppies are enthusiastic about everything; their world is a wonderful place! Take this same approach with your dissertation, think positively; approach each topic area as a challenge, when issues arise, treat them as problems with solutions you can find. The dissertation is a mental challenge; it should push you to try to learn new things.

Puppies are curious about their world, much to their human's concern. Everything must be explored, tasted, chewed on, or played with, whether it is a toy, the cat, or an electrical cord. Take a curiosity view of your dissertation. Keep asking "why"? Why do I think that this will happen? Why did my participants respond in this way and not that? Previous researchers have always looked at the variable from this way... what happens if I look at it from that way? Stay curious about your topic and keep asking questions.

Puppies are very engaged in their world, every moment they are busy exploring, tasting, and trying new things. You want to be engaged in your dissertation in a similar way. Always, you should be considering how the project ideas fit with other areas of your life. When you hear people mention a similar topic, listen in and hear what their views are. Yes, make some time to sit and work on the paper every day, but also play with it at other times, when you are on the bus or train, when you are waiting in line or on hold. Keep engaged in your dissertation.

Giving Thanks

Let us take a moment to think about how saying thanks relates to your dissertation. As a dissertation student, you have come so far in your education! The doctorate is considered the terminal degree, meaning, there are none higher. Just making it to the point of working on the dissertation is a great achievement, take a moment, and realize how far you have come!

Only 4% of the population has a doctoral degree, you are very privileged, you are bright and capable, or you would not have gotten this far. Think of all of the faculty who have given you their time, effort, and wisdom to help you get here... they stretch out far beyond graduate school... all the way to high school, elementary school, and kindergarten. Send them blessings.

Think about all of your classmates and friends who have helped you reach this point. All of the people who have shared your frustrations and your joys, who have been there for support. Send them thanks.

And finally, think about your family members who have given up so much for you to achieve this goal. They have given you time to work, held you in crisis, and celebrated with you in your accomplishments. They may be your cheerleader or your silent supporter, but you know they are behind you. Take a moment to let them know you appreciate them.

Giving Back

When you are in the midst of a high stress situation, such as your dissertation (along with work and family) it is difficult to even consider doing things for others. However, I feel it is important for you to consider a few low-time ideas to give back to others. Why? Think of all of the people who have helped you in your educational process, from teachers, to family, to friends. They have given you their time, their wisdom, and their faith in you, it is time to pass it on.

Here are a few suggestions. Take a few minutes to write three short emails. Send one to someone who has supported you in your graduate program (ideas: teachers, peers, family, or friends). Tell them what they did that showed their support. Tell them why it has been important to you. Then send the other two emails to other dissertation students you know who could use a little support. Remind them what they are doing is important and you believe in them.

Why did I decide on the ratio of one to someone who has supported you and two to people you can support? While it is important to thank those who have helped us, I believe it is even more important to help others. The minute you take to support a friend or peer will make their day; it may be what keeps them working on their dissertation instead of doing something else clamoring for their attention. You may provide the motivation to keep them from quitting when it gets difficult.

You have been given so many gifts; sometimes it is hard to remember it, because it is easy to take them for granted. You are intelligent and determined, how do I know? Because you are working on your dissertation, you would not be here if you were not both of those things. I believe you can get your dissertation done, and receive your doctorate. I believe someday soon you will be able to have Ph.D. after your name, and people will call you doctor. Just keep writing!

Celebrating Small Milestones

It is very important to acknowledge and celebrate the small milestones in your dissertation progress as well as the big ones (e.g., defenses, IRB). What are the small ones? Having your prospectus accepted, completing sections of the paper, having your chair approve chapters. You can even break them down further, with reaching your goal for a week or a day.

Think of each small step as a goal you have completed on your journey. Celebrating them will give you an emotional boost and increase your motivation to push on. How to celebrate them? Perhaps you can think of a range of celebrations and rewards depending on how big the step is; a dinner and movie out with your favorite person for completing a chapter. Maybe going for a long walk or getting ice cream with the kids for reaching your goal for the week. Your reward should be something that is worth working toward that would make you happy and relaxed.

The dissertation is such a long and difficult journey; you need frequent rest stops and rewards for each step on the way. I think it is a great idea to include your significant other and family in your celebrations. It will allow them to be part of your journey and to support you.

Where Did I Put My Motivation?

Do you feel sometimes like you have lost your motivation? Here are some ideas to help you find it again. Do you have a dissertation journal? If not, now is the perfect time to start one, write down how you are feeling, try to determine what exactly is bothering you, do you feel frustrated? Are you feeling overwhelmed? Describe why and how it makes you feel. Then the important next step is to write down why you originally started this process. What led you to be in graduate school and working on your dissertation? What led you to select the topic you did? Now you need a plan, how will you work through your current emotions to get to where you want to be? If you need help with this, your chair should be a great resource. You need a definitive plan to move forward! Get a dissertation coach (this does not have to be formal, a friend or mentor can be in this role, set weekly goals and be accountable to your coach).

Another suggestion is to use affirmations to help keep you going. Something like: "I am intelligent, creative, and capable, I will complete my dissertation and be Dr. (your name)." Tailor it to fit your needs. Then say it to yourself frequently. Write it out and post it near your computer, make it your current life's motto.

A final suggestion is to use visualization regularly. Picture yourself graduating, putting on your cap and gown, and walking on the stage. See yourself receiving your doctoral hood and being called doctor!

Courage and the Dissertation

One does not generally think of courage when considering dissertations, however, it is an integral part of the process. It took great courage for you to decide to move from the path you were on, to that of a doctoral program. You may have left on the old path, friends and even family members who did not understand your new direction. That can be painful and lead to second thoughts. You left comfort and went into the unknown, an exciting but also frightening decision.

You have probably questioned the decision many times, wondering if you are "good enough" to finish. While this is normal, it is also takes courage to face your deepest fears and continue. Along the way, you have had your writing (and maybe your ideas) criticized and had to rewrite, yet you have bravely continued. Today, reflect on your courage and the example you are to others. Because of your example, your children, grandchildren, friends, and people you do not even know may find the courage to face the unknown in order to find a better future. Today, celebrate courage. You have earned it!

Juggling

Life is about juggling multiple things at the same time. The dissertation adds in several additional dimensions to your juggling act. Let us consider these. When writing the dissertation you have to set time aside when you work on the paper without many distractions, this can be difficult with a family. It is also long term, which means planning activities, whether work or family related can be tricky. During the dissertation, you will find that it tends to dominate your thoughts to the determent of other activities, along with this, your family and friends will probably get tired of hearing about it.

How do you keep all of the dissertation "balls" in the air, along with work, family, etc.? First, realize you are one person and can only do so much, you are going to need help juggling! Do not try to keep doing everything yourself, have your family help with household tasks and errands. Get some dissertation support through peers and your chair. It may help to speak to your work supervisor about cutting down on overtime or extra assignments.

Realize there are going to be times when you simply cannot do everything, and you will need to prioritize. If you have a family or health emergency, you may need to take a leave of absence from your dissertation. It is ok (just do not forget to come back to it!). Be realistic about what you can and cannot do, if you are feeling stressed then stop and evaluate. Know your own stress symptoms, take care of yourself and your family, and get help to keep all of the balls in the air!

Sabotage

Are you sabotaging your dissertation progress? Do you find everything in the world to do other than writing? Do you feel you just have to clean that thing which has been sitting there for 6 months, and cannot wait a moment more? Do you convince yourself it is ok to visit your favorite websites instead of the library?

How to get back on track? First, I suggest some self-reflection. It is worth taking some time and thinking about why you are doing these delaying tactics. What it is you are really avoiding? Is it facing an empty page? Or maybe it is the reality that you may get done with your doctorate and have to figure out the rest of your life? Only you can understand the issues.

Consider for a moment, all of the years you have spent working toward your degree, all of the money you have spent. Are you willing to let a paper stop you from reaching your goal? If you are worrying about the post-graduation steps, than begin doing some research in that area (but limit it, writing is more important!). One strategy many find helpful is to set aside 15 minutes a day as official "worry time." Set an alarm so you know it will not last long and make a list of everything worrying you. If there is something, which can be done now, write out a brief action plan and timetable for it. Then set the worry list aside knowing it will be there tomorrow, so you do not need to spend any more time on it.

A few recommendations for specific issues, if the dissertation process is concerning you, read:

Rudestam, K, J. & Newton, R.R. (2007). *Surviving Your Dissertation: A Comprehensive Guide to Content and Process.*

If it is the writing process, read: Saltzman, J. (1993). *If You Can Talk You Can Write.* If you want to know about postgraduate jobs, see your professional organization's website. Most have a career section, including job postings. Only you can make your goal happen, take control of the path to get there.

Making Mistakes

How do you handle it when someone calls you on a mistake you made? Perhaps you inadvertently went out of the line of command on an issue or you did not give credit when it was appropriate in your paper. How you handle these situations is important to both how others and how you perceive yourself as a professional. The temptation may be to deny any wrongdoing, or blame it on other people. My advice is to admit you made a mistake, you will learn from the incident and you will make sure it does not happen again. Be an adult, face the consequences, and move on.

Everyone makes errors; it is the cover-up that causes problems.

Sharing

I have heard a number of students say that have posted information about their dissertation on their personal website or on social media. I caution you to reconsider doing this before the study is complete. The reason is that there are people who may "borrow" your ideas and publish a study on the same topic before you can get your study done. This could mean having to rework your study (remember you are required to make a new contribution to the field). While I do not recommend being paranoid about this (e.g., fearing that your committee will steal your ideas), do be cautious in sharing. General topics are fine, but don't be specific about it.

Are You On The Right Path?

How do you know if you are on the right path in getting a Ph.D.? How do you know if your study or your dissertation is "good"? The reality is you do not know, all you can do is keep going, one step at a time. You will get a lot of feedback and advice along the way to your Ph.D., some you will be required to take to continue, other advice you will have to make your own decision about whether to use it or continue in the same direction. Do not let the decision making lead to a fear of movement, rarely is any decision fatal or unresolvable. One step at a time… keep going.

There is a tendency for many people to become paralyzed in the dissertation process because they look at the big picture and have a hard time seeing themselves making the trip to the end. Focus on the next step, if it seems too big break it down even further. Is writing the first chapter the obstacle? Start with an outline of all the topics you see as related to the topic. Pick one and start reading and taking notes. Is the data analysis freaking you out? What is the first step that needs to be done? Entering the information in SPSS? Maybe transcribing the interviews? Take the first step.

For many students the freezing in the headlight moment comes when they get a committee member's review and yet more changes are required. I recommend reading the review then setting it aside for a day. Resist the temptation to start criticizing yourself, everyone has revisions, this is just another hoop to jump through. Instead, think of it as a problem to solve. Lay out how you will approach it, and take the comments one at a time and address them. No, you do not have to take every suggestion or comment, but you do have address each of them. So if you disagree, use track changes and respond to the reviewer why you have chosen to not change the item. Also, realize the committee member may disagree with you and insist on the changes. Is this thing really worth holding up your progress? If you answer no, then change it, and move on.

Some students get hung up on the idea that their dissertation is "theirs" and they do not want anyone else's advice and refuse to make changes. Please, give up on this idea. It is not "yours" it is your dissertation committee's paper and you are just a member of the committee. Your committee's names will be on the paper as well as yours (check out the dissertation database, if you want to see). Their job is to make sure your paper will get through the process, do not waste time with ownership issues, move on. Trust you are on the right path, trust your mentors, and keep taking one more step to your goal.

One Step Forward, Two Steps Back

Sometimes research feels like you are not really making progress... you read over the paragraph from yesterday and wonder "what was I thinking?" You discover an article with a study almost exactly like yours. Your chair (committee member) wants yet another revision. How to keep going?

First, realize while these setbacks are maddening, they are also a normal part of the process. It happens to everyone. The difference between the person with an ABD (All But Dissertation) and a Ph.D. is the second one keeps going. Yes, you will have days that feel like you are going backward, but you will also have days when you plunge ahead and make progress. Keep going.

Second, know you are not alone you have help available; just reach out. Your committee and your peers are all available. Let us consider for a moment how best to approach them. Despite the strong temptation, do not whine, complain, and blame the world. Say what is going on and what you are looking for from the person. Here is an example to a peer:

Hi Mindy,

Like you, I am working on my dissertation. I find I am really having problems keeping motivated, would you be interested in being a dissertation buddy with me? I am thinking perhaps we could commit to contact each other once a week or so and offer encouragement. It might help me if I felt accountable to you to get something specific done each week. What do you think?

Jane Student

Recognize they may say no, and that is ok. But if they do say no, have someone else in mind to ask. Keep going until you find the person you need. You are the only one who can find you the support you need. It is an important element, which may make the difference between your being ABD or having a Ph.D. after your name.

Third, I find it very helpful to set a goal for the week and each day with my writing. What is realistic? Maybe five pages a week? Only you know what would be reasonable for you. However, make yourself a commitment and stick to it. You will be shocked at the progress you will make. Be sure to allow time for editing, it a very important element of writing and will save you time in the end.

The Power of Habits

Have you ever thought about your dissertation in terms of a habit? We know in psychology that connecting a specific cue and behavioral routine to a reward reinforces the behavior. Let us consider this in terms of your dissertation. If you set up a positive cue with working on your dissertation, say an early morning cup of special coffee that you love, with sitting down to write, over time, you will begin to link the smell and taste of this positive coffee experience with the routine of working on your paper. Let us add in an additional reward of feeling the reduction of anxiety and stress over your paper. If you consistently have your special favorite beverage only when you work on the paper (set a time requirement – maybe an hour?), and then pay attention to your reduction in anxiety, you will soon have a winning combination!

Make a daily habit of writing at a specific time when you feel fresh and have the quiet time to work on the paper. Link it with something you particularly love, perhaps special music, drink, small snack, etc., make sure this is only time you have access to the positive reward. You will soon find the experience to be one you look forward to doing.

Negative Habits and Your Dissertation

Previously, I discussed how to create a positive habit related to your dissertation, now we consider what negative habits you may already have created within yourself. Close your eyes and visualize sitting down to work on your paper, notice how you are feeling. Do you sense anxiety? Do you have any negative feelings that may be leading to procrastination? If only positive feelings are present, congratulations! Run along and work on your paper! However, if you did experience any negative feelings, hang around and let us talk for a moment.

To state an obvious point: you are engaging in self-defeating behaviors and you need to figure out some ways to stop them. I have some suggestions for you; get the book The Power of Habit: Why we do what we do in life and business by Charles Duhigg (2014). Begin setting up some positive associations between your dissertation and things you love, what those associations are, is up to you (the book can help), but you want to create an atmosphere of excitement and pleasure to come to mind with your paper. If you have had some bad experiences with your paper, this may be influencing things, take positive actions to correct them. Some suggestions: find someone you know who was an English major and writes well, ask them to help you edit your paper or hire an editor. Consider taking a writing course. Do Something! Take positive action and break the negative cycle.

Ordinary Days

"A (hu)man can stand anything except a succession of ordinary days." (Goethe)

What is an "ordinary day" for you? Do you keep to a rigid schedule of family/ work/ dissertation, juggling everything at once? Does it all begin to seem so difficult that you want to crawl into a dark corner and escape? Perhaps it is time to plan a little break. Do not panic, I am not suggesting a long expensive trip (although wouldn't that be nice?), rather a half day of doing something you love to do and getting away from your ordinary days.

What could you do? Perhaps you could take a short trip to a favorite local place (the beach? A museum? Coffee house?), have the rule that no thinking about work/ dissertation is allowed. Perhaps what sounds the best is some time to work on a favorite hobby or read a trashy novel. Take the time to give yourself a small gift of extraordinary. It will remind you why you are putting yourself through all of this work, to change your ordinary present days to an extraordinary future.

Guilt

It is common to feel guilty when you are not able to work on your dissertation. You may feel you are letting yourself and your family and friends down. One student described it as a "chronic experience of 'not enough'. Not enough progress today, not enough extant literature to support my point, not enough energy to write..."

How can you use these feelings to help yourself instead of letting them drag you down? One way is to establish a realistic schedule of working on your paper. Decide that as long as you are keeping to your schedule you are doing all you can, and you do not need to feel guilty. What is realistic? An hour or two a day is probably a realistic goal. If you have a hectic work schedule, you might want to think about it terms of a weekly number of hours. Yes, reading articles while in waiting rooms counts! The main thing is to try to quantify it and keep track of your time. That way you know when you can give up the guilt reminders.

Think of guilt as a reminder from your subconscious. Deep down you really want to get your doctorate; this is so important that you are making yourself feel guilty about it. This is a good thing! However, take control of the guilt and use it to its best advantage. Do not allow the guilt to become so overwhelming that you avoid working on the paper in protest. Put working on the paper on a strict schedule, so your subconscious is happy and stops sending out alarm signals of guilt.

The other side of this issue is to allow yourself some time away from your paper. Give yourself permission to not work and think about it at certain times of the day/ week. You will find you come back to it with more energy and creativity. As you consider your daily and weekly schedules, add in time for you and things you enjoy doing. Give yourself rewards of time off, "if I work on the paper for 2 hours today I can go to a movie (take a walk, spend time with my kids/grandkids, etc.)."

Working Through Your Guilt

"I feel so guilty if I am not writing every day." This is a common experience for students, but is it a valid concern? Personally, I would like you to expand "working on your dissertation" beyond simply writing. The dissertation requires many tasks, including literature searching, reading, filing, organization, and simply thinking about the study. All of these tasks are important and all take time to do. I suggest you try something for the next week: lay out what you really need to do on your dissertation, what tasks are needed? Be explicit. Your list might look something like this:

Check literature on gender and self-efficacy in the library, print articles
Read at least 5 articles and notate them
Write and edit 3 pages on gender and self-efficacy
Update references on the pages written
File the articles
Update research journal

Now lay out what you will try to accomplish each day. Perhaps your week will look like this:

Monday - Check literature on gender and self-efficacy in the library, print articles. Update research journal

Tuesday – Read and notate 2 articles, write about the key points for each article. Add references. Update research journal

Wednesday - Read and notate 2 articles, write about the key points for each article. Add references. Update research journal

Thurs. - Read and notate article, write about the key points, add references. Update research journal

Friday – Read through writing for week, edit and clarify writing. File articles for the week

When you have completed your tasks for a day, you can stop feeling guilty! If you have a lot of work/ family/ personal issues this week, take those into account and adjust your work plan accordingly.

Success

Success is the sum of small efforts, repeated day-in and day-out. (Robert Collier)

This quote is the essence of working on a dissertation: small efforts, small steps, doing a little something every day. Sometimes life seems to overwhelm and it seems impossible to work on your dissertation, but remember this quote and do a little something on it; file some papers, read an article, just think about your project, perhaps consider your theory and what it predicts.

Every day do something on your dissertation, sit and write for an hour, read articles in the waiting room or while you are waiting for someone. You can do this... one small step at a time. In the next chapter, I explain how to start your proposal.

Health Issues and the Dissertation

Life has a way of throwing things at you when you have the least time for it. This makes sense from a health psych perspective, as your stress increases, the chances of health issues increase proportionately. So let us talk about how to handle health issues during dissertation work.

As you probably know, there are two types of illnesses: acute and chronic. Acute illnesses are short term ones, such as colds, flu, a broken bone, etc. The key point is that they are time limited, there is an end in sight. For these types of illnesses, keep your chair informed of the issues. Do not just disappear from dissertation! Faculty members understand that emergencies happen, but make sure they are informed as soon as possible. Let your chair know if there are issues that will affect your writing ability, a great example is a student with a broken wrist. He or she may be able to use voice recognition software to write, but it will definitely slow the progress. Remind your chair occasionally that you are dealing with this, they may not remember. Contact disabilities services to cover yourself. You may want to let your dissertation peers know for support and suggestions.

Chronic illnesses are more of a challenge. Chronic illnesses are ones that are not time limited, they may continue indefinitely. Some examples are diabetes, multiple sclerosis, and some forms of cancer. Contact disabilities services – they may be able to offer extensions and other accommodations. Let your chair know about your issues, it may be a good idea to educate them a little on your illness so they understand what to expect in the future. It is a good idea to give your chair info on how to contact your next of kin so they have a way to check up on you if you disappear from the classroom (you must give permission to allow such communication). It is also a good idea to give your next of kin your chair's contact info so they can update him or her. Remind your chair occasionally that you are dealing with this illness, they may not remember.

If a flare-up or crisis occurs, you may wish to explore taking a leave of absence (LOA) with your academic advisor and chair. Ask about what it will mean with your dissertation. Can you return and be with the same chair? Consider LOAs if you are going through a difficult period, do not risk getting an unsatisfactory. Be sure you keep in contact with chair during LOAs, he or she needs to know that you are ok and your plans for the future. When you return from your LOA, let your peers and chair know how you are doing. Remember, these people have formed relationships with you; they can be supportive if they know what you are dealing with.

Is an Outside Mentor for You?

I have had a couple of questions about whether having a mentor outside of education is useful. First, let us define what we are talking about; it is NOT someone on your committee. We are talking about someone in your field of interest that might have an applied view of the topic. This person may be able to offer insights that from the applied side that you cannot get from just reading about the topic. An example might be if you are interested in domestic violence, a contact or mentor that works in a shelter may offer ideas that you have not considered.

It is definitely something to consider, but a few cautions- remember they probably do not know what is required for a dissertation in your university, so do not rely on them for this type of advice. Even if they have a doctorate, they probably do not have the necessary knowledge of your university's dissertations. Always check their comments/ ideas against the literature; they may have interesting anecdotal information, but you must rely on empirical support. An applied perspective can lead you in interesting directions; however, it must be tempered with literature.

How do I see the relationship working? Talking with them when you are trying to come up with a research question makes sense. Running ideas that you find in the literature by them may be useful. Also when you have your results talking them through in light of their applied experience may be very helpful. Just keep in the back of your mind that you are not trying to please them, they are not on your committee, use them as a resource.

It is a nice idea to send them thank you notes for helping you and a printed bound copy of your final dissertation. Be sure to mention them in your acknowledgements.

CHAPTER 7
THE DISSERTATION PROPOSAL

You have had your project ideas approved by your committee, and given the okay to begin your dissertation proposal. Great! So what exactly is a proposal?? The proposal is the first three chapters of your dissertation. It lays out the research plan for your study, the literature basis for the project, and the theoretical implications. It also demonstrates your ability to think through the study and show yourself to be an expert in the content area. At this point you probably do not feel like an expert; however, keep in mind one of the purposes of the proposal is to develop your expertise. You will do this by conducting and writing a full literature review and by carefully developing and writing the methodology for your study.

The proposal aspect of your paper is very important in the sense that once your committee has approved this document, you are confirmed as ready to progress to your study. No further changes are expected. However, you should plan to go through the first three chapters, after your defense, and change all verbs relating to your study from future ("X will be done...") to past tense ("X was done...").

Starting to Write Your Proposal

How do you start your actual dissertation proposal (chapters 1-3 of the dissertation)? First, I want you to read a few things to make you feel more comfortable. Begin by reading your institution's dissertation guide. This will walk you through all of the many rules that go with the dissertation. Next, go to the library, find the dissertation database, and go through a few recent dissertations from your institution. See if there are any related to your topic, but also look for a similar methodology. You might also want to look at one for which your chair was the chair. You do not need to carefully read them, but get a feel for how they are laid out; look at how the student wrote the literature review. Save them all on your computer, you will want to look at them when you are stuck on a section.

Many institutions now have a dissertation template, which lays out the formatting and required headings, check if yours has this. Look through the first three chapters of the template (if you do not have one, make your own with headings based on the recent dissertation you downloaded), this will be your proposal. I hope you are beginning to feel a little more confident!

I strongly recommend that you begin writing your proposal with Chapter 2, the literature review. This will help you understand what has been done previously in this area and how it has been approached. Start with a new Word document; copy in everything from the dissertation template's chapter 2. You should now have a good idea of the direction you need to go. Go ahead, name the file, and add the date in the file name.

I always recommend you develop an outline of the topics you want to cover in your literature review (I provide an example Chapter 2 outline in Appendix D). Start with broadest topic then work down to the narrowest one. Make sure all of your variables are included in your outline. What topic do you feel you already know the most about? Start writing on that topic, there is no reason for you to start at the beginning of the chapter. You will eventually have to fill in all of the sections of your outline, but first build up your confidence a little.

Once you have a draft of the first section of chapter 2, ask your chair to look at it for you. Pay attention to the feedback you get; does your chair mention APA issues? Look them up in the APA manual; try not to make the same error again. You might want to start your own checklist of common writing problems you have, so you can always remember to check them. Does your chair say you need more evidence? This is a common issue. Think of it as you are building a case for your argument; support each step. Do not assume your reader knows anything about the topic: educate them! As you begin writing your proposal, I would like you to keep in mind the concept of resilience.

Resilience

Have you heard of the concept of resilience? It is defined as reflecting the characteristics of inner strength, competence, optimism, flexibility, and the ability to cope effectively when faced with adversity (Wagnild & Young, 1990). This concept came to mind when my dog, Maggie, had to have a kidney removed due to cancer. Within 3 days, she was up and active, enthusiastic about life. That is resilience!

How does resilience apply to a dissertation? This is a long-term project often taking more than a year to complete, it will push you to your limits… in a sporting metaphor this is an ultra-marathon not a sprint. You will need to be tough: enduring criticism, learning new concepts, and coping with adversity when it arises. You will need to be optimistic and stay focused on the positives not the negatives. You will need to believe in yourself.

Take a few moments now and think about why you are getting your doctorate. To get a better job? Fulfill a lifetime goal? How important is it to you to do this? You are tapping into the basis of your resilience. That feeling of commitment will help carry you through the rough times. How to remember it? I suggest getting a photo or small token, which reflects your goal. I remember for me it was a little toy red sports car that symbolized making my own money and choosing my own car. No, I did not get a sports car when I was done, but I did get a red Saturn sports coupe I dearly loved.

What symbolizes your goal and commitment for you? Find something and put it where you will see it every day. Remember resilience: inner strength, competence, optimism, flexibility, and the ability to cope effectively when faced with adversity. I know I believe in you. You can do this!

What is Resilience?

A general definition of resilience (Cooper, Flint-Taylor, & Pearn, 2013) is "being able to bounce back from setbacks and to keep going in the face of tough demands and difficult circumstances, including the enduring strength that builds from coping well with challenging or stressful events" (p. 15). That definitely sounds like something, which is needed for writing a dissertation!

There are a number of characteristics associated with resilience found in the literature, including the capacity to accept and confront reality, ability to find meaning in life, ability to improvise (Coutu, 2003), hardiness, commitment, control, and challenge (Maddi & Khoshada, 2005). Military based studies have indicated resilience is an ability to bond with a group with a common mission, having a high value placed on altruism (unselfish concern for others), and the capacity to tolerate high levels of fear and still perform effectively (Charney, 2004). Other positive factors include optimism and conscientiousness. Factors not related to resilience are chronic anger and hostility, neuroticism, negative affect, and having a socially dominant style (Smith, 2006).

I hope by now you are convinced that resilience is a strong asset in completing a dissertation. Next, I will discuss some ways to build resilience and apply it to the dissertation process.

Building Resilience: Positive Mindset

Let us consider how you can build resilience through a positive mindset. You can learn to see and interpret the world positively; however, I am not saying that if you want something enough and really believe in yourself you can make anything happen. This is simplistic thinking, and there are other important elements to consider, such as talent, opportunity, encouragement, focus, hard work, resilience, and luck. The challenge is in finding the skills and techniques that help you maintain a balance between the extremes of negative thinking and naïve positive thinking.

People who habitually see "problems as threats" undermine their resilience, in part because their bodies are continuously experiencing adrenaline and cortisol associated with stress and negative emotions. This results in their bodies being in constant alert, ready to deal with perceived and actual threats.

In contrast, an achievable challenge is seen as a potential source of satisfaction. Broadly speaking, one can look at the world in two ways: as a threat or as a challenge. Persistent negative thinking often results in a pattern of negative consequences that can be self-fulfilling, and as a result people become trapped by their automatic thoughts in response to a situation, thoughts that make them feel worse and less able to cope. The first step in correcting negative thinking is to recognize automatic negative thoughts and their possible consequences. Here is a brief list of common automatic negative thoughts, and likely consequences, together with alternative more positive ways of thinking about the same situation.

Automatic reaction	Consequence	Alternative
I will never get done	Takes longer to complete	I will get done if I take it step by step
There is no point in trying	Won't even try to do something about it	There is always a way
My chair hates me	Does not interact with chair	Let's see if I can understand my chair's point of view. If that doesn't work out I will try to find another chair.

Building Resilience: Increasing Optimism

The main quality possessed by resilient people is an optimistic outlook. Optimists tend to see their problems as short lived, changeable, and specific to circumstances. By contrast, disposition or habitual pessimists see their problems as permanent, persistent, and pervasive. Pessimists tend to blame themselves for setbacks and failures, where optimists tend to look elsewhere for the reasons or causes. Some people seem to be born with the gift of optimism but extensive research studies have shown that optimism like helplessness can be learned.

The first step in increasing optimism is to begin disputing pessimistic assumptions. The steps to doing this are:

Describe a recent disappointment or event as specifically as possible. Describe how it made you feel about yourself and your role in the event. Now answer the following questions

What are alternative ways of viewing the event, especially ways that are changeable, specific to circumstances, and not personal to you?

What is the worst-case scenario? How bad is it really?

What are the consequences of holding on to this negative belief about you?

How do you feel about it now?

Here is an example:

Setback: Chair wants another revision

Emotional response: this kind of thing always happens to me. I must be a terrible writer.

Evidence: remember the times when your writing was accepted. What is the evidence that this always happens to you? Think of your successes and when things were going well. What is different now?

Alternative viewpoints: I can get some writing help from my friend who was an English major. Can I see this as an opportunity? Perhaps I need to rethink how I am approaching my writing.

Consequences (of holding onto the pessimistic thoughts): become passive and negative. Increase the likelihood that I will be unable to write. Feel frustrated.

Feel now (consequences of changing thinking): less helpless, more ready to take charge and manage this.

Building Resilience: Re-Framing Problems

Re-framing is a cognitive technique you can learn so you can begin to see the possibilities in situations that previously had been seen only as problems. Below are examples of problems, and how they can be reframed into more creative options and opportunities. It is important to note, you need to work out a new perspective that is realistic, believable, and helpful for you. Others can suggest positive perspectives, but these will not make any difference unless they are relevant and meaningful to you.

Problem	How Can I Reframe It?
My chair wants to resign from my committee	What opportunities might be there? Could I find someone more interested in my topic? How can I make the experience better in the future?
I am getting an Unsatisfactory this term	What challenges does this present that I could rise to? How can I learn from this? What should I do differently? How can I show my true strengths?
I hate to write	How can I get pleasure or satisfaction out of it? Could I streamline or systematize the process? Could I learn to like it? Can I set myself challenges to meet?
A mistake you made	What can I learn from this? What led up to it? How can I avoid repeating it?

It can be hard work to find the alternative thoughts that work for you, but it is well worth the effort as the results can be life changing.

Building Resilience: Avoiding Common Thinking Errors

The way we think about things is a strong influence over our emotions. Consider the common thinking errors described below.

1. *All or none thinking.* Are you seeing the problem in black and white terms? (Example: My chair wants revisions to my dissertation, I'm a terrible writer).

2. Are you looking at it in a too narrow way, for example focusing on only the negative comments made by your committee and ignoring other important aspects?

3. Are you *jumping to conclusions*, assuming you know? Do you have all the facts? Do you have any facts?

4. Are you *exaggerating or minimizing* the real picture? How does it compare to others? Have you checked? Are you keeping things in perspective, taking a balanced view?

5. Are your *emotions/ fears holding sway* over your reasoning? Are you reacting emotionally? What are the facts? Is the language you are using mostly emotional rather than factual?

6. Are you *boxing yourself into a corner*, where you see only one option? (Example: if my chair did not respond to my e-mail then I am certainly not going to write to her again).

7. Are *you labeling people and things* in more extreme terms than they deserved or stereotyping them? (Examples: I'm a disaster. They are lazy.).

8. Are you *blaming yourself* for things that are outside your control? (Example: I should have known better than to pick this committee).

Recognizing the thinking errors is the first step to avoiding them. Over time it is possible to learn helpful alternative thoughts that avoid these errors and let you stay on a more positive and realistic track.

Building Resilience: Reflection

A habit of reflecting on the present and recent past can have a powerful effect on how you see and cope with the present and the future. Questions to ask yourself regularly include:

What did I do related to my dissertation today? This week?

What went well with my dissertation today? This week?

What did I enjoy?

When did I feel my best?

What did not go so well, why?

How can I avoid that, change it, think about it differently?

What can I do to get more positives into my dissertation this week and fewer negatives?

To get even more from these reflection questions, write your responses in your research journal. This gives you the opportunity to go back over time, look at how things have changed, and monitor your growth and development. In the next chapter, I begin going through the dissertation from beginning to end.

CHAPTER 8
DISSERTATION CHAPTER 1: INTRODUCTION

The Beginning Pages

A look at a completed dissertation or your template will show you there are a number of pages before you actually start on Chapter 1. Let us begin our examination of the full dissertation with the title page. First, will be your title. It needs to be less than 12 words; it should include your variables and the population of your study. Under your title comes your name, you should give some thought as to how you want your name written. You may wish it to match your doctoral diploma.

Next, you will list any previous degrees and the institution from which you received them. There is then some standard wording of your degree. Finally, you will list your institution and graduation date.

The Abstract

The abstract is one of the most important aspects of your dissertation. It will be listed in dissertation abstracts and will be read by people interested in your study in the future. It should be under one page and describe the key elements of your study. These elements include the gap in the literature you are addressing, your population, the theoretical framework for your study; the methodology; general procedures; analyses, and when your study is complete, the results and implications of the study.

Keep in mind, you are not allowed to use citations nor should you spell out numbers even if they start a sentence. I recommend this be the last thing you write both for your proposal and for your final dissertation. The next page in your dissertation will be a repeat of the cover page.

Optional Pages

Next are some optional pages if you wish to include them. First is the dedication page, in which you may dedicate your dissertation if you wish. On the following page, are acknowledgements. This gives you the opportunity to thank the people who helped you complete the study. Common acknowledgements are to your committee, family, and often to the people who participated in your study.

Table of Contents Pages

The next set of pages is your table of contents. Students often have a difficult time formatting these. If you are fortunate enough that your institution provides a dissertation template, it will help a great deal. If you must build it yourself, be aware in Word under the References tab, there is a table of contents button. Use the help menu to set it up. Following the general table of contents, there is a list of your tables and a separate list of figures.

Chapter 1

Chapter 1 is the official beginning of your proposal; it is a very important chapter in that it sets up the reader to understand an overview of the study and to appreciate the need for it. You will find it is actually easier to write Chapters 2 and 3 first, then do this chapter. When you are ready to begin, start with a typical outline:

Introduction
Background
Problem Statement
Purpose
Research Questions and Hypotheses
Theoretical and Conceptual Framework
Nature of the Study
Definitions
Assumptions
Scope and Delimitations
Limitations
Significance
Summary

I am sure the first thing you notice is there are many sections; each of these will be quite short, think of them as concise summaries.

Considerations: Introduction

I think it helps to think of this first chapter of your proposal as an introduction to your study. It is not considered a continuation of your abstract, so you need to repeat information given in the abstract.

The introduction to Chapter 1 is one of the most important parts of your entire paper. This is where you grab your reader's attention and provide a map of where you are going. You need to explain very concisely the need for your study (the gap you are addressing). This is where you might want to include a few statistics showing the size and concern of the problem. Give enough background literature to put the study into context, and explain briefly what method you will use. By the end of the introduction, your reader should understand what the gap is, how you will do your study, and why your study is needed to fill the gap you mentioned.

The introduction is a difficult section to write, because it needs to be two to five pages. The language needs to be clear, without jargon, and to the point. Do not write in "academic" language; at least initially, write to your grandmother, explaining it in normal language. If you must use any terms that might not be known to your grandmother, define them. Avoid using acronyms if you can, I hate having to have a cheat sheet to translate many abbreviations. Have some friends or family members read the section and ask them questions about it. Why am I doing the study? How am I doing it? Do you get the feeling my study is needed?

Theory

Joe asks: I am a bit unclear about the development of a theory for a dissertation. Is it required, or is the development of hypothesis(es) adequate? When developing a theory, when should the theory be introduced, in the prospectus, before the research, or after the research has been completed and analyzed? Finally, can a good theory in the social sciences still be probability based? For example, theories starting with "People will generally..." or "it is more likely that..."? One more while I am on a roll :) For the purposes of a dissertation, does every aspect of a proposed theory have to be tested by past research or research in the dissertation? For example, can a dissertation theory make a prediction that might be suggested by previous research but has not been tested?

Many questions, Joe! First, you are not required to develop your own theory in a dissertation, and I would strongly discourage a student from doing so. Developing a theory is difficult and requires validation with multiple studies. Instead, consider modifying an existing theory AFTER you have analyzed the data. So you could say something like "Theory X predicted A and B should have occurred in the present study. However, A and C occurred, perhaps theory X needs to be modified to allow for such outcomes."

A good theory should lead to predictions and be testable. This is the problem we see with some of the older theories, they cannot directly be tested (an example is Maslow's theory of hierarchy of needs). So, I am not

73

sure how to answer your probability question, most theories could be considered probability ones in that they would not be correct 100% of the time.

The purpose of including theories in the dissertation is to see what they predict and how your results fit those predictions. Think of it as validity testing, if your results were very different from the predictions, then the validity of your study is in question. In addition, absolutely, a dissertation can test aspects of a theory not previously studied.

Theoretical Foundation vs. Conceptual Framework

From Deb: I have a question regarding the difference between theoretical orientation and conceptual framework. I know for qualitative research, generally speaking, the framework is used. However, my chair thinks it is a good idea to use both. I am all for it, but try as I might, I am having difficulty wrapping my head around the two enough to articulate them. Can you make clear the distinction between the two? Please and thank you :-)

Great question, Deb! A theory is usually found in the scholarly literature and has been formalized and tested by other researchers, it should explain relationships between variables. Theories are often multilayered and complex. A conceptual framework is a less developed form of a theory and consists of statements linking abstract concepts, in psychology it is often described by the term "model." Keep in mind that a conceptual framework is NOT the type of qualitative study you are proposing in your study (e.g., phenomenology). Here is an example of a conceptual framework I developed examining online faculty work satisfaction.

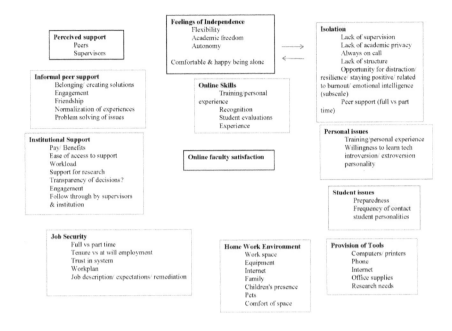

This is a way to lay out your variables and how you think they interact, as opposed to a theory, which is more refined and has aspects, which may have been previously tested. If you would like more information on conceptual frameworks, take a look at Ravitch and Riggen's (2011) book: *Reason & Rigor: How Conceptual Frameworks Guide Research.*

Research Questions

What are research questions? These are general over-arching questions about the topic and should include your variables of interest. They are not interview questions and they are not hypotheses. Research question(s) are the foundation of the dissertation. Everything done in your dissertation should relate to the research question(s). Research questions will generate hypotheses in quantitative studies and provide a framework for methodology in qualitative studies.

The research question should not be:
- Too narrow ("What is the mean number of ...")
- Too broad ("What is the effect of loneliness on the elderly?")
- A question that is not researchable ("Is helping behavior selfishly or unselfishly motivated?")
- A yes-no question (Does parental divorce cause depression in

children?)

One way to develop research questions is to read the literature in your area of interest, and then to brainstorm (in your research journal) ideas about your topic and how variables might interact. Consider an example of older adults (people over 65). I am interested in their satisfaction with their physicians. What might be factors that would affect the interaction? I read the literature in this area and then brainstorm some ideas: perhaps length of time spent with the physician, maybe the physician's expression of empathy, and perhaps the age and gender of the physician could be factors. Some possible research questions about these might be:

How does the amount of time spent with the physician affect patient satisfaction?

How does physician empathy affect patient satisfaction?

How does the physician's age influence patient satisfaction?

How does the physician's gender influence patient satisfaction?

Some things to notice about these questions, they are not hypotheses (a hypothesis might be: as time with physician increases, patient satisfaction increases). They do not predict how you hypothesize the results will come out. They lead to some issues related to the research method; for example, I will need a way to determine patient satisfaction and physician empathy.

Rudestam and Newton (2007) provide three questions to determine if your research questions are appropriate (p. 20).

1) Is the question clear and researchable, and will the answer to the question extend knowledge in your field of study?

2) Have you located your question within a context of previous study that demonstrates you have mastered and taken into consideration the relevant background literature?

3) Is the proposed method suitable for exploring your question?

Definitions

Part of Chapter 1 is a section on definitions; you would think this would be simple! However, even this section has some rules you need to know. First, every definition needs a citation. Do not use Wikipedia for your source. Second, you should not use the word you are defining in its definition (e.g., "Older adult: an older adult is..."). Third, your definitions need to be in alphabetical order.

Which words should you define? Any words or terms that are jargon and may not be known to the average reader. Do not include statistical tests or theories here. This section is where you would define terms related to your population that may have multiple meanings ("older adult," "young adult," "baby boomer"). Terms you are using in a specific way should be listed here ("online education," "synchronous learning," "homelessness," domestic violence," "faculty mentor").

Do not define acronyms here; that should be done in the text, the first time it is used. An example: "The lexical decision task (LDT)..." Per APA 4.21, remember to italicize key terms on first usage, often this will occur in the definition section.

Assumptions

In this section, you need to clarify aspects of the study which, as the researcher, you believe to be true but cannot demonstrate their truth. Some examples: you assume your subjects will be truthful in their responses. You assume your participants are appropriate representatives of your population of interest. You assume any survey measures (e.g., a measure of self-efficacy) you are using adequately capture the variable of interest.

Scope and Delimitations

The Scope section asks you to describe specific aspects of the research problem that are addressed in the study and why the specific focus was chosen. Let us use a silly example, you are examining adults' fear of pencils in public settings, such as a library. You need to explain why you decided to examine adults (as opposed to other age groups) and why public settings, as opposed to other settings.

In Delimitations, define the boundaries of the study by identifying populations included and excluded. Think about this section in terms of generalizability (or transferability in qualitative studies), to whom will your findings generalize? This section makes you tightly consider your true population and sample. Let us consider an example. If you are doing an online survey study of parents' opinions on bullying, only people with access to a computer will be included. Think about how you are recruiting your sample, as an example let us say you are posting an announcement through Facebook, only parents who access that Facebook page will be included. Another thing to consider is probably only people with strong opinions either positive or negative will choose to participate. Therefore, in this example, your true population (and delimitations) will be parents who have access to computers, see the ad posted in Facebook, and who have opinions strong enough to motivate them to join your study.

Limitations

The limitations section asks you to consider your sample and its similarities and differences from the population. Unless you carefully sample thousands of people, your sample will not be representative of the population, which is fine. You just need to be aware of how your sample will differ from your population. Consider racial and cultural differences between your sample and the general population. Other things to consider are people who volunteer to be in a research study are probably different from those who do not volunteer, so that is a limitation to mention. Think carefully about your recruitment and research methods, how will you recruit? Who will not be included? Will you hand out flyers in a doctor's office? Then people who do not visit the doctor during that time will be excluded. Again, all of this fine, it is just part of research, but it is important to understand the study's limitations.

Nature of the Study

A section students are often asked to revise is the Nature of the Study. This section can be thought of as an overview of your project. It begins with a rationale for selecting the design or tradition you will use. Questions to ask yourself are: why is this the best method to use to answer my research question? Why are other methods not appropriate?

You will then need to summarize your research methods. Go into some detail here, how will you recruit your participants? How many people will participate? In general, what will happen to them in your study? How will you analyze the data you collect?

If you have not written Chapter 3 at this point, it can be a difficult section to write. If you must write Chapter 1 first, I suggest thinking of this section as a placeholder, put in what you think you will do and plan to revise after you have written Chapter 3. This section should force you to begin thinking through your study, remember Chapter 3 should be in enough detail that someone could replicate your study based on the description. Therefore, this is a good place to begin considering the details. You should try to imagine how each step will work: How will you recruit? Will you use a flyer or ad? What it will say and look like? Where will it be posted? What will people who wish to participate do, in order to be included in the study? What happens then? How will you get their consent to participate? Every detail will need to considered and addressed in Chapter 3, so begin now to work through them.

Significance

This section, I addressed in the prospectus and the same issues need to be addressed in Chapter 1. The significance section informs the reader why your study is needed. You need to "sell" your idea and convince the reader it is necessary.

Describe how this study will contribute to filling the gap you identified in the problem statement. What original contribution will this study make? Keep in mind that is the main criterion that determines whether your study is of "dissertation quality."

Discuss how your research will support professional practice or allow practical application. This part should answer the "so what?" question. Why do we need this study?

Discuss how the significance you have highlighted aligns with your problem statement to reflect the potential relevance of this study to society. This is getting at the bigger picture: How might the potential findings lead to positive social change? Use the "4Ds" as you think about the social implications: death, disabilities, disease, and dollars.

Chapter 1: Summary

Students often treat the Chapter 1 summary as a last minute add on, however, it is important in its own right. In the summary, you should briefly review the main points from your chapter and talk about what will be discussed in future chapters. Why do you have to do chapter summaries? The dissertation should not be looked on as a "paper," it really is a book you are writing. Just as a textbook has summaries at the end of each chapter and a preview of the next one to keep the reader interested, so should your dissertation.

Playing the Waiting Game

Waiting is an essential part of the dissertation experience. You wait for faculty to review your paper and wait for IRB; every person has time to review it. Why does it take so long? What should you do while you are waiting so the time is not wasted?

Why does it take so long? Typically, the time is not spent in just reviewing your paper that actually just takes a few hours. The problem is faculty may have many more students and other obligations, they may be traveling and attending conferences, or be on vacation. So the waiting time is taken up with getting to your paper.

What can you do to use the waiting time productively? You can go on to the next step, such as the next chapter, working on the PowerPoint for your defense, or the IRB application. You can do an updated search in the library, seeing if there is more recent literature you can use; check the dissertation database and other databases outside your field. You can work on organizing your workspace, filing system, or learning new software such as EndNote. You can read some reference books on your method, statistics, or theory.

The important part is to keep working on something related to your dissertation! Do not just sit there doing nothing, use the waiting time productively. This is your paper, take ownership, take control, and get done!

Thinking about Chapter 1: Lucy

Visualize a future reader of your paper, a doctoral student named Lucy. Lucy is thinking about doing a study on a similar topic to your dissertation and wants to learn more. We will follow Lucy's thoughts on your completed paper through each chapter of your dissertation. As you write your paper, think about Lucy reading it in the future, your dissertation is your message to her.

Chapter 1 is the introduction to your paper and has quite a few sections that are needed to prepare Lucy to understand the rest of the paper. It begins with a general introduction, by the end of this section Lucy should have a good understanding of the gap in the literature your study is addressing and why you are doing this particular study. Next, you briefly bring Lucy up to speed on the key literature in the background section, again you are just introducing the gap in the literature; it should not be a terribly long section. Now bring in your problem statement. There should not be any surprises here. The problem statement should be a succinct statement of the needs you are addressing, so Lucy knows if you and she are considering similar problems.

Your research questions and hypotheses are important information for Lucy; they tell her what you are studying, the measures you will use, and how you will interpret the results. Next, explain to her your theoretic7al framework, make sure she understands why you have chosen that theory and how you see it applying to your study. The Nature of Your Study will explain to Lucy the method you will be using and the population and sampling strategies you will use.

The next section will educate Lucy on the terms you will use in the paper, make sure you explain anything she may not find familiar and give her citations so she can read further, if she wishes. The assumption section tells Lucy what your beliefs about your population and study are before you started it. The scope and delimitations tell her what population your study will generalize to and to whom it does not generalize; this lets her know if she can cite your study in hers and if it can be seen as a direct link to hers or just a related one of interest. The limitations section tells Lucy about any methodological weaknesses you were aware of and any biases; explain to her how you tried to take reasonable measures to address them. Finally, the significance section lets Lucy know what you see as the applications of your study, regarding the overall discipline, practice, and social implications.

Whew, you have taught Lucy a lot in this chapter! By the time she finishes reading it, she should have a good understanding of what you are doing in your study and why you are doing it. She should, of course, be impressed by the clarity of your writing and thinking, and impressed with your grammar and formatting. You have set a high bar for this future doctoral student to reach! In the next chapter, we will move on to the literature review in Chapter 2.

CHAPTER 9
DISSERTATION CHAPTER 2:
LITERATURE REVIEW

You have done some literature searches and have piles of articles. Now what?? First, as discussed in the writing chapter, make an outline of Chapter 2 (there is a full example of an outline in Appendix D); include the information provided in the template or the recent dissertation you downloaded. You will see there are a number of required sections in Chapter 2, including an Introduction, your search strategies to find your literature, the theories you are using, main concepts or philosophy of your method, and the literature review itself. Within the literature review, you will need to go into depth on each of your variables, including the history of the topic, research methods used previously, previous findings, a description of what is missing from previous research, and what your study will add to the literature. You will also want to discuss each of your survey instruments, with what populations have they been used previously, and in what contexts they have been used. Finally, you will provide a chapter summary and your conclusions.

There are a number of approaches with this type of writing. One is to start off with a brain dump of everything you know off the top of your head, then go back and find empirical support and add citations. This works well if you have been reading a lot in the area or you have a background in this area. Whether or not you have this background then you need to begin general and work to the specific on the topic.

One of the best ways to approach the literature review is to take an historical approach. In this approach, you trace the development of the concept through time. For example, if you are interested in resilience in the elderly, you would want to see first when resilience begins showing up in the literature as a variable, then when it begins to be applied to the elderly.

You would then want to discuss the various ways it has been examined in the population and what the research has reported. By the time you are done, the current state of the literature should be clear to the reader.

Start your outline by thinking of the broadest category of your variables and work down to the narrowest. For example, if you are interested in older adults and their opinion of their health care provider (one of my own research interests). You would want to start with aging and the elderly, providing demographics, what constitutes "elderly," and discussing the importance of the age group. Then move to elderly and health care, showing why this is an important topic. Next, the elderly and their health care provider. Since this is the narrowest category and the key area of interest, you will want to discuss this in more depth. You will particularly want to address how this area has been examined methodologically. Next, you will discuss each of the survey instruments, examining their previous use with the age group, and in the context of health care. If anyone has examined the relationship of the surveys with health care providers, you will want to include this too. Here is the starting outline for the chapter, and my notes:

I. Introduction
II. Search Strategy
III. Theories
    A. Theory A
    B. Theory B
IV. Concepts/ philosophy
    A. Info on my methods, philosophy behind it
V. Literature Review
    A. Aging and the elderly, include demographics
    B. Elderly and health care, why do we care about topic?
    C. Elderly and their health care provider
        1. Include methods used previously
        2. Previous findings
        3. What is missing from previous research?
        4. What does my study add?
    D. Survey instruments
        1. Survey A
            a. Used with my age group?
            b. Used in health care research?
            c. Used in health care providers research?
        2. Survey B
            a. Used with my age group?
            b. Used in health care research?
            c. Used in health care provider-related research?

VI. Summary and Conclusions

You will refine this as you search the literature and bring in related areas; but to begin the chapter you now have some direction. Once you have an outline you should consider sending it to your chair for feedback, is there anything else he or she thinks you need? Now start writing; with which of your topics on the outline do you feel the strongest? I suggest starting on that topic. Use your research journal to keep track of your starting outline and any notes to yourself as you go. I am a big fan of track changes and include comments to myself in the paper as I write (e.g., "find more about this topic," or "check Smith et al. paper, did they say this too?").

I have a tendency to find interesting but tangential literature, which can lead me far from my topic; the outline keeps bringing me back to task. Think of it as a map of where you are planning to go.

I recommend adding in your references as you go, otherwise, you will spend several long frustrating hours later trying to track them down. Prevent plagiarism by never copying into your paper. Instead, read the passage you are interested in, and restate it in your own words (including your own old papers). Avoid quotes, saying it in your own words is always better.

Relate Everything Back to Your Study

It is important to remember every section in your literature review needs to relate back to your study. Are you including the variables/ issues in your study you discussed in a specific section of the literature review? Why or Why not? Keep reminding your reader how topics relate to your study and why they are important elements. If you cannot relate the topic back to your study, you probably should not be including it.

Come and Look Over My Shoulder: Literature Review

I have been asked to write a literature review as an article in a journal for midwives and doulas. I thought you might find it helpful to "look over my shoulder" as I select a topic, do the literature search, and organize and write the paper.

The journal editor asked me to pick a topic on the subject of child obesity that would be relevant to childbirth educators (e.g., midwives and doulas). I start by doing a search in the library in PsycInfo, CINAHL (a nursing database) and Medline. I like to start searches as narrow as I can; I want to link child obesity closely to pregnancy, since that is the readers' interest, so I start with the search term infant obesity. I find a variety of topics, many focused on interventions and assessments; I read through the titles and abstracts. One topic that particularly appeals to me is the relationship between maternal obesity and child/ infant obesity. My next step is to make sure there is sufficient literature in this area to write a literature review on the topic. I do a search using the terms maternal obesity and infant obesity, hmmm, only three articles. I try the terms maternal obesity and child obesity. There were a number of articles on this, so I narrow it further and add in the term review, which will find me any previous literature reviews of the subject, and there are three recent ones.

My next step (at least my typical next step) is to go to an online bookstore and search for any reference books on the subject. I search using maternal AND child obesity. There are a couple of books on the topic, they have the tables of content available, so I double-check and yes, there are chapters on the topic (I add the books to my wish list to save them for now). I now know there is a reasonable literature available on the topic. Now I double-check whether the editor is interested in the topic. I send her an email and yes, she likes the topic.

I go back to the library and extend the search to maternal obesity and long-term effect. I also run the searches again in the Psychology Sage database. I download any articles that seem appropriate and save them on the computer, I end up with 10 articles. I also go back to the online bookstore and buy the best two books on the subject. I will probably need more articles when I start to write, but this is enough to get me started and familiar with the topic area.

How did the process I went through relate to your dissertation searches? Mine was a smaller version of your literature search. You can start with the same basic search technique to find a topic: (a) Discover whether there is sufficient literature for your proposed topic. (b) Start very narrow in the search and then broaden it. You will have specific variables you are interested in, so include those as you broaden the search. (c) Download (or print) your articles and be sure to check if there are reference books available on the topic.

Come Look over My Shoulder: Organizing the Paper

I have read the literature I downloaded earlier and am now aware there are several key issues: the effects of obesity on the mother in pregnancy and childbirth, the effects on the fetus and newborn, and long-term effects on the child. There is evidence from both human studies and animal studies related to the child issues, so I want to make sure I address both of these areas. My initial plan, depending upon how long the paper is at this point, is to end the paper with a brief discussion of weight gain in pregnancy and summarize the research concerning interventions to reduce maternal weight gain during pregnancy in obese women.

I like to begin writing a paper with a title; that way I can keep focused on where I am going. My starting title is: The Effect of Maternal Obesity on the Development of Child Obesity. I then do an initial outline:

I. The effects of obesity on the mother in pregnancy and childbirth
II. The effects on the fetus and newborn
    A. Human Studies
    B. Animal Studies
III. Long-term effects on the child
    A. Human Studies
    B. Animal Studies
IV. Weight gain in pregnancy
V. Interventions

A first look, tells me I am going to be way over the 12 pages I am allowed if I include all of this. Therefore, I think I will add a very short discussion of weight gain to the mother topic and leave out interventions. I will concentrate on human studies, but may mention a few animal ones. My starting outline then for writing is:

I. The effects of obesity on the mother in pregnancy and childbirth
    A. Weight gain in pregnancy
II. The effects on the fetus and newborn
    A. Human Studies
    B. Animal Studies
III. Long-term effects on the child
    A. Human Studies
    B. Animal Studies

I like to set up my paper in APA format before I actually start writing; it lets me feel like I am not staring at a blank page. So next, I will write out the cover page info, add page numbers, label the Abstract page (I will write this last), and add the title to my page 3, which will be the first page of the manuscript. I also add in my references as I write, so I set up a page for that.

My next step is to write an introduction, which I know I will probably change later. I want something that will grab the reader's attention and also give me focus as I write. I end up with this intro paragraph.

Marie is pregnant with her first child, at a weight of 200 pounds and with a height of 5'6" her body mass index (BMI) is 32, which is considered obese according to the Centers for Disease Control (CDC; 2011). How could her obesity affect her health during pregnancy? How could her weight affect her baby and are there long-term implications for her child? This article will explore these issues.

How does the process I went through relate to the writing of your dissertation? You need to decide what the key issues are before you begin writing; otherwise, the temptation will be to wander away from the topic. Most people have this problem (including me!), so put guides in place to keep you on track. This is the purpose of doing an outline, and thinking about the topics to cover before you start writing. The penalty for not doing this is you may write many pages only to realize they have absolutely nothing to do with your topic. Setting up your paper in advance, may help you avoid the paralysis of a blank page. Writing an interesting introduction grabs your reader and lets them know where you are going in your paper. Finally, I find it helpful to keep reminding myself that nothing is permanent when I am writing; I can and probably will change it later.

Come Look over My Shoulder: Writing

Rather than give you my actual writing, I think it may be more helpful to explain why I am approaching it in a certain way. The first section from the outline was:

I. The effects of obesity on the mother in pregnancy and childbirth
   A. Weight gain in pregnancy

I previously discussed starting your literature review broadly and narrowing it as you progress, which I will also do my paper. I want to present a case during my review, that the issue is real and should be of concern to the reader. Therefore, I will carefully lead them in this direction. First, I need to educate the reader on terms and definitions of what I will be discussing. I will start with explaining what I mean by obesity, and give some definitions. If I have any quotes, it would be in this section. This paper is for practitioners (midwives and doulas), any guidelines as to how to recognize obesity I provide will be useful for them in their practice.

I want to show obesity is first an issue in the United States in general, so it would make sense to look at some statistics from the National Institute of Health (NIH) or the Centers for Disease Control (CDC) demonstrating the importance of the issue. Then I will narrow the topic to obesity and pregnancy, I need to show how many women fit this category. This is also where I will discuss what a normal weight gain is during pregnancy and what is abnormal. I will discuss the interaction of pre-pregnancy obesity and weight gain during the pregnancy. What are the major health concerns during pregnancy for obese women?

Again, I want you to notice I am guiding and educating my readers, do not assume they know anything about the specific subject. Assume your readers are intelligent and experienced in their field, but do not use jargon. They can always skip over information they already know, but you cannot go back and fill in knowledge they are lacking. Do not feel the need to write "academically," typically such a style comes across as difficult to follow and makes the reader have to translate it; instead be logical, define terms, and guide them in the direction you want them to go.

Next in my paper, I will look at the issues related to obesity and childbirth, how does it complicate giving birth? Again, my focus is on the mother, I will switch to the child in the second section. I keep reminding myself as I go, why do we care about this issue?

I always enter citations/ references as I go, and make notes when I need to find a citation to support a statement I have made. Remember any facts you state must have a citation. I also make notes (using comments in track changes) of areas that need more literature or need additional support from the literature.

Once I have a section that seems to be taking shape, I start the editing process, rereading and clarifying. I will start my next writing session by rereading what I wrote the last time and seeing if it still makes sense. Have I missed any steps in my logical argument? Have I led my reader to the point I wanted to make in the section, that obesity is a serious issue for the mother during pregnancy and childbirth?

How does my writing relate to your dissertation? You also must educate your reader, build a logical argument, and demonstrate why your reader should care about the topic. As, potentially, a future reader of your paper, I beg you not to try to write "academically!" Your paper should be a careful balance between writing professionally about a technical subject and avoiding the use of the thesaurus just to impress. It does not impress me using convoluted language; I really prefer to understand what you are saying.

Reading Research Articles

How do you read research articles? I think everyone develops their own system, but here are a few suggestions. Decide what you want to know from the article before you start reading. Are you trying to get general information? Are you concerned with methodology? You may not need to read the entire article, but only pieces to get the information you need. Be very careful about simply taking their discussion comments as the actual results of the study, writers often over-interpret their results, so check them yourself.

Develop a shorthand or marking system. Whether you read your article in a pdf form (on the computer) or a paper version, you should be developing a method to keep track of important information. I tend to read pdfs using software such as ReadCube or Mendeley, so I highlight in yellow the key points I want to be able to find again. I also write myself notes in the article about why I think the highlighted text is important (e.g., "interesting qualitative method," "confirms my idea on self-efficacy in this population"). If you are reading the paper version, you can add sticky notes marking important issues (consider color coded ones, e.g., pink = method issue). Have a master list of what your codes/ colors mean so you remain consistent.

You may want to keep an Excel file of articles with key points for each article you read. An alternative is to use bibliographic software such as Endnotes, and make comments in the entries. The trick to all of these is to be consistent in using and maintaining them. Decide on how you want to read articles, in pdfs or in paper version and set up a filing system to work with your method.

Reading Articles: Literature Reviews

What should you look for in articles' literature reviews? I will give you a few general guidelines; I suggest highlighting or marking each of these areas in your article. The areas may not be specifically labeled, so it often takes some detective work. For each area, consider how it relates to your study. Are you examining a similar social problem or gap in the literature? Is this a theory that would be applicable for your study?

First, find the social problem being addressed in the study. In other words, what is the big picture reason they are doing the study? Determine what gap in the literature the study is filling. This is looking at the specifics of what has been previously done and how the study fits into the history of the topic area. What theory/theories are the authors utilizing to address this issue? How do they integrate the theory into the study?

What are the study's research questions? What are they planning to examine and how does it relate to the literature gap?

What are the study's hypotheses? They may use language such as predictions or expectations. Also, examine the variables of interest within the hypotheses. Are they using survey measures? What type of scores or sub scores will result from the measures? Have you ever heard of the measures they are using?

Reading Articles: Method Sections

Determine what overall methods were used to answer the research question(s) (e.g. quantitative, mixed methods, interviews; observations). Then determine what specific design/type of quantitative method was used (e.g. experimental, quasi-experimental, survey, etc.) or what qualitative method was used (e.g., narrative; case study; phenomenology; grounded theory; straight qualitative)?

Next, examine which specific individuals or animals constitute the population? Be specific (e.g., adults between 65-85 years, who live in the Midwest and attend senior centers). Who is in the sample and how were they recruited? Is the sample appropriate to the identified population, or did the recruiting methods, reduce the study's population? For example, did the individuals have to use a computer? Then the study is limited to those who are willing/ able to use one. What is the sample size? How was the sample size determined? What measures are used and are they valid? If interviews were conducted, are the interview questions appropriate to answer the research questions?

Reading Articles: Results and Discussion Sections

The results section of articles, are often the one students want to skip. However, it is important to read this section and keep in mind a few things. Highlight significant results ($p < .05$); for each one, write in your own words what it means (e.g., females had higher self-efficacy than males). Does it make sense they used the type of statistic or qualitative method that they did? It is a good idea to compare the author(s) original research questions to the results they provide; do they address each question? Look at whether any qualitative data were quantified to answer the research questions.

When you are done with the results section, compare your notes to the authors' discussion points. Do they interpret the results differently than you? How do they relate the results to the literature and the gap they were addressing? Do you agree they have resolved the questions? Make notes as to what you agree and disagree with.

Finally, take a look at the references for the article, are they reputable journals? Do the authors only seem to cite themselves? Pay attention to the how old the references are; are they recent? You may want to make note of which ones you would like to read.

You have now learned to review articles! Once you have your Ph.D., you may be asked to be a peer reviewer for journals, and this is the method you will use to do so. Take notes, so you do not have to reread the article several times.

Updating Your Literature

Students often feel that once they have completed Chapter 2's literature review they do not have to look at the literature again. Sorry, not true! I suggest every month or two, during your waiting for faculty time; you go to the library and update your literature. New articles are constantly being published, and you want your literature review to be up to date. Do you need to do an exhaustive search each time? No, but you may want to set up a schedule, so over several months you have checked on all of your variables and theories.

Then add in the new articles into your literature review. I suggest using track changes, so it is obvious to your faculty reviewers what is new information and what they have previously read. Keep track of your searches in your research journal and if you find new info. It will make it much easier to remember what you have done along the way if you keep a map through your journal. Remember that you should be an expert on the literature related to your study, so keep reading!

Chapter 2: Lucy

Your future dissertation reader, Lucy, is ready for Chapter 2. She begins by reading your introduction, which sets the stage for the rest of your literature review. Briefly remind her why you are doing your study, give an overview of the literature review and the main sections of your chapter, this is helping her to see where you are leading her. Next is your literature search strategy, this section is important to Lucy, because it gives her a map of how you went about the literature search. It tells her what databases you used and the search terms used. If she would like to follow up on your study, she will need to retrace your path.

Your theoretical framework section is where you teach Lucy about your theory and how you are applying it. Make sure she follows your logic by laying it out carefully. Discuss the history of the theory and how the theory has progressed over time. Relate the theory back to your study and how you see your methods being influenced by the theory.

The rest of the chapter will be examining your variables: their history and how you see the variables interacting in your current study. It is very important to indicate to Lucy your logic of including each variable and how it relates to your study. Assume that while she is very intelligent, but she may not have any knowledge of your topic areas, so explain them thoroughly. Keep bringing each topic back to your study and how you are examining it. By the time she has finished Chapter 2, Lucy should have a full grasp of the literature related to your study and a clear understanding of the need for your study. Of course, she should still be impressed with the clarity of your writing and formatting!

Thinking About Your Audience

A student question:

How do you remove yourself enough from your dissertation to put yourself into the readers' shoes so to speak, so you can tell if a proposal covers everything necessary?

This is a good question! You want to assume your audience is intelligent and knows generally about your field, but has no knowledge about your topic. Think of it as educating your readers. Explain terms, tell them the background of your variables, and do not assume they know anything about it. Put yourself in the position of the instructor, be thorough, and explain.

I also want to reassure you that this is exactly what your committee will be helping with. They will tell you when you need more explanation and description. A common comment is "define this," or "go into more detail here." In the next chapter, we will move on to Chapter 3 of your dissertation, the research methods.

CHAPTER 10
DISSERTATION CHAPTER 3: METHODOLOGY

Chapter 3 is an important part of your proposal; it will detail what you are actually doing in the study. Let us begin by seeing what is in the dissertation template, note each of the research methods has a different set of requirements. I suggest beginning your draft by writing down each of the requirements for your study, some examples are:

Qualitative

Introduction, Research Design and Rationale, Role of the Researcher, Methodology, Instrumentation, Data Analysis Plan, Issues of Trustworthiness, Ethical Procedures, Summary

Quantitative

Introduction, Research Design and Rationale, Methodology, Instrumentation, Threats to Validity, Ethical Procedures, Summary

Mixed Methods

Introduction, Setting, Research Design and Rationale, Role of the Researcher, Methodology, Instrumentation, Data Analysis Plan (for both quantitative and qualitative), Threats to Validity, Issues of Trustworthiness, Ethical Procedures, Summary

Chapter 3 is going to be much trickier to explain than the previous discussions, because each research method has slightly different requirements. I am going to try to address all three research methods' sections. I will clearly indicate to which research method it applies. You may find it helpful to read the chapter in this book on Data Collection at this point, as I give some pointers on the various methodological choices.

Setting (mixed method)

First, to be discussed is the Setting section. In this section, you describe where you will be collecting the data and why this setting is appropriate and relevant to your study. Describe the aspects of the setting that will affect your study, some examples, are geographical location and the size of the organization, indicate how these aspects will affect your study. Think in terms of replication, if someone wanted to replicate your study, what should he or she know about where you did your study?

As an example, if you were going to do a mixed methods study of online students' opinions about variable X, using the participant pool of an online university; you would describe it as a large online university (you would not give specific names of organizations). Your reader would want to know how many students attend the university and any information you could gather about the participant pool. Then you would want to discuss why this university is a good choice to examine your topics.

Research Design and Rationale (all research designs)

This section introduces the research design of your study. Each of the types of design has slightly different requirements for this section.

Quantitative

Begin by restating your research questions (from Chapter 1); indicate which of your variables are independent, dependent, moderating, etc. Then clearly state the type of research design you will be using, an example, might be a 2 (gender) x 3 (age: 20-30, 30-40, 50-60 yrs.) x 2 (time 1, time 2) repeated measure design. Which means, in this example, you will have an equal number of males and females; equal number of people from each of the age groups, and each person will be tested more than once. Relate the design to your research questions.

Discuss how your choice of designs makes sense with what is needed to advance the literature. Perhaps, a great deal is known about the variable, gender and people's age at a single point in time. However, your design allows a look at how things might change over time by testing them at two time points.

Qualitative

Begin by restating your research questions (from Chapter 1). Then describe the main concepts you will be addressing. Next, you will discuss the research tradition you are using, some examples include phenomenology, case study, narrative, etc. Provide a rationale for using that tradition. Why is the one you chose most appropriate for your study? Why not use one of the other traditions?

Mixed Methods

Begin by restating your research questions (from Chapter 1). Then describe the main concepts you will be addressing. You then need to identify how you are using a mixed method and how the data collection and analyses work together. Discuss how this is the best approach to answer your research questions, and why you need to use both quantitative and qualitative elements. Finally, discuss why you have chosen the analysis method you will use and how you will be analyzing the data.

Role of the Researcher (qualitative and mixed methods)

In qualitative and mixed methods, you need to discuss your role as the researcher. Why? Because you are going to be doing the interviews, therefore, who you are and how you know and interact with the participant is essential to understanding the study.

You will first define and explain your role as an observer of the behaviors, a participant in the interview, and /or an observer-participant. Next, discuss any relationships you have with the participants, particularly if you have a supervisory relation (this will be a big issue for the IRB, so think if there is a way around using your supervisees).

Next, you will discuss how your own biases will be managed. Every researcher comes into a study with biases, if you did not have ideas as to what you thought would happen, you would not do the study! You may have been (or are) a member of the population group, how will you keep that from influencing your interview? You will need to be impartial and unbiased, how can you do this? One common way is to approach subjects/ participants neutrally and keep a journal where you relate any emotions that come up for you. It is common for new interviewers to want to engage in a social conversation with the participants and share their own experiences. Do not do this! Your story may influence how they respond to questions; you want to approach the topic as someone new to the topic. Do not assume you know what the participants are going to say, let them explain the details.

Finally, you need to think through any other ethical issues, such as, doing a study within your own work environment, conflict of interest or power differentials. Then lay out a plan for addressing any issues present.

Participant Selection (qualitative and mixed methods)

This section, participant selection, is only used for qualitative and mixed methods. First, you need to identify who your population is; it is often a good idea to think about it as who does the study generalize to? Therefore, if you are interviewing victims of domestic violence in your small rural town, your population may be victims in rural areas.

Next, you will want to identify and justify your sampling strategy. There are a number of ways to recruit your participants, a couple of examples are placing flyers in areas you suspect they frequent (do not forget hair salons, barbershops, supermarkets, and churches), another example is snowball sampling where you ask each participant to suggest other appropriate people who might be interested. You need to explain why this is a good method for your study, perhaps you have a hard to reach group and this will ensure a sufficient sample size.

Now state your inclusion and exclusion criteria. Be very detailed, think about who can participate. People who are native English speakers? Able to read and speak clearly? Only people who have been divorced for over a year? Clearly articulate who can be in your study (your inclusion criteria) and also who cannot be in the study (your exclusion criteria). Then discuss how you will know if they meet the inclusion criteria; will you ask them? Do you assume if they can read your consent form they can read English?

How many people will you have participate, why did you select that number? For mixed methods, you will need to go further and indicate how many people will be in the quantitative portion and do a power analysis. How many people will be in the qualitative portion, and how will you select those to be interviewed?

Part of all qualitative studies is the concept of saturation, whereby you continue to sample until you are consistently getting responses you have heard before. You need to discuss saturation and how it relates to your sample size.

Population and Sampling Procedures (quantitative)

In quantitative studies, it is particularly important to understand who your population is and who it is not. Therefore, the first thing to address in this section is: who is your target population. Again, the best way to think about this is to whom does the study generalize? If you are testing undergraduates, that is who your population really is (contrary to many of the old studies who make the case they are similar to the population in general). Next, you want to state approximately how large the population is you are using. This may take some detective work to find.

The next section is Sampling. You rarely can test the entire population; instead, you must strategically sample to make sure you get a representative group. How will you do this? There are many ways that have been suggested, the important thing is to realize the cost and benefit of each method, and how they affect your study. For example, you may decide you will post flyers and have people contact you if they want to participate. There are a number of costs of doing it this way: you will only get people who frequent where you are posting flyers, you will only have people who volunteer, and only people who have a phone to contact you. None of these issues are fatal flaws, but you need to be aware of them. You may want to consider representative sampling, in which you relate your sample to the United States Census in your area. For example, if the Census indicates that you have 20% Blacks, 5% Hispanic/ Latin(o/a), and 75% Whites in your area, you would want your final sample to match these proportions.

What are your inclusion criteria (who can participate) and exclusion criteria (who cannot participate)? Think details. If you are doing an internet survey on survey monkey (this is an online site where you can construct surveys and collect data), inclusion criteria include: people who can read English, have access to a computer, as well as any issues related to your population (e.g., divorced for a year).

You will need to do a power analysis to determine how large your sample should be. Check with your methodologist, as to whether they have a preference as to how to do it. I generally recommend using one of the power analysis calculators available online (do an online search for power analysis calculator). You need to give the website you used for the calculation and why you used the parameters you entered. You may need to talk to your methodologist about this aspect.

Recruitment (quantitative)

In this section, you need to think details! It must be written in enough detail that someone else could replicate the study based on your description. This is always more difficult than you think it will be, you might find it helpful to talk through the section with someone, such as a classmate or spouse. Have them push you for as many details about it as possible.

Start with how you will recruit, will you put up flyers? Send out emails? If you are sending out emails, where will you get the addresses? Make a note you will need copies of all communications (flyers, emails) for the IRB and they will need to be in your paper's appendix. If you are planning to post flyers in or get email lists from a company, organization, institution, etc. you will need a letter of agreement from them describing this.

Once people contact you, what will you say to them? This needs to be written out. If you are sending them to a survey on a website, what will it include? What demographic information will you collect? Typically, you will want to know their sex, age, and maybe socio-economic status. This is collected so you will be able to describe who your sample is. There may be other information you will want to know to confirm their eligibility to be in the study, perhaps marital status, part or full time work, etc.

Each participant will need to read and agree to a consent form (check with your IRB, they probably have a template). If they are completing an online survey, this is usually the first page of the survey. A copy of the consent form will need to be sent to the IRB and be included in your paper's appendix.

Next, you need to describe how the data will be collected. If you are collecting data in person, what exactly will happen? Where will you do it (you will probably need a letter or cooperation with any locations where you do the study)? How will you make sure it is private? Again, be very specific as to how this will occur. Then you need to discuss if you will debrief your participants in some way (often done in in-person studies). This is where you thank them for participating and give them an overview of the study, if it would not have been clear before. Again, a copy will need to be sent to the IRB of the debriefing and added to the appendix. Finally, describe any follow up procedures, such as their being contacted again in the future or having to return for any reason. You should plan to send your participants and any agencies or organizations that helped you along the way a summary of your results (1-2 pgs.), describe how you will do this.

Additional Information (quantitative)

There are three special cases I will examine: a pilot study, conducting an intervention, and archival data. I am a fan of pilot studies (more on this in the chapter on the IRB), but you do need to explain why you are doing one and who will participate in it. Pilot studies are typically done to give you an opportunity to practice your procedures, check the clarity of the measure, and to determine how long the full study will take (so you can report it in your consent form).

Doing an intervention, which means introducing any new training, treatment, or information to your participants, can be very tricky. If you have been thinking along these lines, I caution you to contact your IRB and talk to them about it. Often you, as the researcher, will not be allowed to do the intervention; some other group or institution may have to sponsor it. You may be only allowed to collect the data about the intervention. After you talk to the IRB about this, if it still makes sense to do an intervention, you will need to clearly describe what will be done and who will do it. Also, clearly indicate what your role will be.

Archival (or secondary) data, using already collected data in your dissertation, can be a great method to use (I will discuss this more in depth in the chapter on data collection). You will need to relate all the information about how the original study was done, including recruitment and data collection. Then you need to describe the procedure you will use to access the data, including any permission letters you need (include them in the appendix). If you are using historical or legal documents, describe how you know they are accurate and why they are the best possible sources to use.

Participant Selection (qualitative and mixed methods)

The section on participant selection for qualitative and mixed methods is similar to the quantitative, except you need to think of it in terms of the methodology. So again, identify your population, to whom will the results generalize (transferability)? In qualitative/ mixed method studies the population is generally smaller than quantitative, so if you are interested in women who have been in domestic violence relationships, think about what age range will be included? What geographic area? All of these issues limit the transferability.

Identify and explain your sampling strategy. For example, will you use snowball sampling? How will that happen? How will you do your initial recruitment? Why is this the best method for your specific study? How will you know participants meet your inclusion criteria? Using the previous example, how will you know they have been in abusive relationships?

How many participants do you need? Why did you decide on that number (hint: support it with literature)? For mixed methods studies, you will also need to explain how many participants you need for each aspect, and you will need a power analysis for the quantitative portion. Talk to your methodologist about this.

Carefully describe how you will identify, contact, and recruit your participants. Be very detailed. Remember if you plan to rely on any other people/ organizations for referrals or help in any way, you will need a letter of agreement from them, spelling out exactly what they will do and provide.

In qualitative studies, you need to consider the idea of saturation, meaning when you are not getting any new information from participants. How does this fit with your sample size? If you have not reached saturation by the time you have talked to all of your required sample, what will you do? (Hint, keep doing interviews).

Instrumentation (qualitative)

In qualitative studies, if you are talking to people and not using archival data, you will design most of your instruments. You need to identify each data collection instrument and provide the source of it, if you did not design it (some examples: observation sheet, interview protocol, focus group protocol). There is also secondary data, which would need to be identified as well as the source (e.g., videotape, audiotape, artifacts, and archived data).

If you are using historical or legal documents as a source of data demonstrate the reputability of the sources and justify why they represent the best source of data. Then clearly demonstrate the link between the data collection instruments and your research questions.

For published data collection instruments

Explain who developed the instrument and provide the date of publication. Detail where and with which participant group the data has been used previously. You then need to justify its use in the current study (that is, context and cultural specificity of protocols/instrumentation) and whether modifications will be needed.

Describe how content validity will be or was established (how do you know it is looking at what you think it is?) A common way to do this is to use an expert panel (3-5 people familiar with the topic who are asked to review your study/ interview questions). Discuss any context- and culture-specific issues specific to the population when the instrument was developed. An example might be if you are using an interview protocol that was designed for adults, and you want to use it with adolescents, you would need to change some of the language.

For researcher-developed instruments

What did you use as the basis for instrument development (some examples might be from the literature or from doing a pilot study)? Again you need to describe how content validity will be or was established (how do you know it is looking at what you think it is?). Finally, you want to describe how your instruments will answer the research questions.

Instrumentation (quantitative)

Generally, students rely on previously published survey instruments for quantitative doctoral studies. I do not recommend developing new surveys for a doctoral study. I will explain more on this below.

Begin this section by discussing each instrument you will be using, who developed it and when. Then indicate why you have chosen it, and why it is appropriate for your study. You will need permission to use the instrument from the developer, include it in your appendix. Discuss when and with what populations it has been used and how validity and reliability were established for each study. Then go into detail about the published validity and reliability values (e.g., Cronbach's Alpha), which are relevant for your study (those using similar populations).

If you are developing your own instrument, first describe the basis for its development. Did it come through items indicated in the literature? Do you plan to do a pilot study to refine the questions? You will need to provide evidence for its reliability and validity, this typically requires extensive testing (100s of participants). Finally, show how the instrument will answer your research questions. If you are developing your own instrument, it will require quite a bit of testing and additional work; again, I do not recommend this for a dissertation.

If you are doing an intervention involving manipulation of an independent variable (e.g., a pre vs. post program evaluation), there are issues that will come up with the IRB, address them early! As far as Chapter 3, identify any materials that will be used in the intervention. Indicate who developed the materials and where they have been used previously (you also may need permission from the developer to use them). If you developed them, indicate how that was done.

Next, you need to operationalize each variable. For example, if you are interested in resilience, define it and how you will be measuring it. Then talk about how each variable or score is calculated and what the scores represent. Give an example item from each scale/ subscale.

The final portion of this section is your data analysis plan. Mention what software you will use, how you will clean the data (how you will handle missing data, and make sure there are not any extreme outliers; see the quantitative analysis chapter for more details). Restate your research questions and hypotheses from Chapter 1; for each hypothesis describe the statistical tests that will be used. If you are doing multiple statistical tests, you need to account for that by using a correction statistic (Bonferroni's correction is common, it reduces your p value, based on the number of tests). If you are using covariates and/or have confounding variables, you need to discuss it. Finally, how will you interpret the results (key parameter estimates, confidence intervals and/or probability values, odds ratios, etc.)?

Instrumentation (mixed methods)

For mixed methods, the instrument section has to accommodate both qualitative and quantitative instruments. For the qualitative components, identify each instrument (observation sheet, interview protocol, focus group protocol, videotape, audiotape, artifacts, archival data, and other kinds of data collection instruments). State the source of each item and provide the permission for it in your appendix.

For published instruments, identify who developed it, where and with what populations it has been used. State why you think it is appropriate for your study and any cultural or context issues that might be present with your population.

If you are designing qualitative instruments, explain how you developed them: what was the basis for them? How will you establish content validity (an expert panel is often used)? Similarly, for the quantitative components, explain the background of each instrument. Discuss validity and reliability in previous studies and where it has been used before. The next section is how you will recruit participants for each component (qualitative and quantitative). Go into detail on how and where you will be recruiting your participants and how the data will be collected for each component.

Finally, you need to lay out your data analysis plan for each component. For the quantitative aspects, indicate your hypotheses and what statistical tests will be used for each. How will you interpret the results? For the qualitative portion, indicate how you will code the transcripts and how you will handle discrepant cases. Then you need to integrate the two types of data and compare their results. How will you do this?

Threats to Validity: External Validity (quantitative and mixed methods)

External validity is the extent to which the researcher can conclude that his or her results apply to a larger population (generalizability). Here are some common threats to external validity.

Reactive or interaction effect of testing. A pretest might increase or decrease a subject's sensitivity or responsiveness to the experimental variable. In other words, giving a pretest changes your participants, they will respond differently later because they took the pretest.

Interaction effects of selection biases and the experimental variable. You may unintentionally choose people that have particular biases. For example if you are doing an online survey about use of the internet, you will probably only have people participate who are already comfortable enough with the computer and internet to choose to participate in an online survey. You will be missing people who are not comfortable with computers.

Reactive effects of experimental arrangements. It is difficult to generalize to non-experimental settings if the effect was attributable to the experimental arrangement of the research. So, if you are doing some type of experiment in a controlled setting (picture a quiet psychology lab room), there is no way to know what will happen when a similar occasion occurs in the real world.

Multiple treatment interference. If multiple treatments are given to the same subjects, it is difficult to control for the effects of prior treatments. People cannot "unlearn" something, so whatever has happened to them previously will affect future learning/ experiences.

In this section of Chapter 3, you need to think about the threats to external validity in your study. Keep in mind no study is perfect, it is ok, in fact, it is expected that there will be issues. The important thing is you recognize them, and do what you can to correct them.

Threats to Validity: Construct and Statistical Validity

A construct is an attribute, proficiency, ability, or skill that happens in the human brain and is defined by established theories. For example, "resilience" is a construct. It exists in theory and has been observed to exist in practice. Construct validity has traditionally been defined as the experimental demonstration that a test is measuring the construct it claims to be measuring. Such an experiment could take the form of a differential-groups study, in which the performances on the test are compared for two groups: one that has the construct and one that does not have the construct. If the group with the construct performs better than the group without the construct, the result is said to provide evidence of the construct validity of the test. An alternative strategy is called an intervention study, wherein a group, which is weak in the construct, is measured using the test, then taught the construct, and measured again. If a difference is found between the pretest and posttest that difference can be said to support the construct validity of the test.

There are a large number of threats to construct validity, too many to discuss here, but I do suggest that you take a look at http://www.socialresearchmethods.net/kb/consthre.php when you are ready to write this section. The author does a very nice job laying out the many types of possible threats.

The last issue is statistical conclusion validity. Statistical conclusion validity is the degree to which the conclusions about the relationship between your variables based on the data are correct or "reasonable". This is getting at the two types of statistical errors that can occur: type I (finding a difference or correlation when none exists) and type II (finding no difference when one exists). Statistical conclusion validity concerns the qualities of the study that make these types of errors more likely. Statistical conclusion validity involves ensuring the use of adequate sampling procedures, appropriate statistical tests, and reliable measurement procedures. If you would like a more in depth discussion of this topic, please see http://www.socialresearchmethods.net/kb/concthre.php.

Issues of Trustworthiness (qualitative and mixed method)

Rather than issues of validity present in quantitative studies, qualitative (and mixed methods) have trustworthiness issues. The first issue is credibility, which is comparable to internal validity. This is getting at the credibility of your data, common methods used to address this issue are triangulation, prolonged contact, member checks, and saturation. You want to show that your data are as accurate as possible.

The second issue is transferability, which is comparable to external validity. This is getting at the generalizability of your data to other groups. Common methods used are thick description and a variation in participant selection. Thick description (Geertz, 1973) is a highly detailed account of the interview locale, interviewees, and actions identified. Variation in participant selection is referring to representatives of all type of people in your population, varying in gender and race/ ethnicity as appropriate.

The third issue is dependability, comparable to reliability. You want to show the accuracy of your data method; common methods are audit trails, triangulation, and member checks. Audit trails means keeping a detailed record of everything done in the study, whom you met with, and what was discussed. Triangulation is accomplished by asking the same research questions of different study participants, by collecting data from different sources, and by using different methods to answer the research questions. Member checks occur when the researcher asks participants to review both the data collected by the interviewer and the researchers' interpretation of the interview data. Participants are generally appreciative of the member check process, and it allows the study participants to fill in any gaps from earlier interviews.

The fourth issue is confirmability, comparable to objectivity. Confirmability is the degree to which the findings are the result of the focus of the study and not of the biases of the researcher. One way to do this is through an audit trail. An adequate trail of records should be left to enable someone else to determine if the conclusions, interpretations, and recommendations can be traced to their sources and if they are supported by the inquiry.

If you are using another coder(s), you must show how you will demonstrate inter-coder reliability. Inter-rater or inter-coder reliability is used to reduce bias by having multiple people code the data. How you go about this and how you resolve any discrepancies needs to be detailed.

Ethical Procedures

For the ethical procedures section, you will begin with stating what agreements you have received to get access to your participants or your data. An example might be if you are interviewing people through an agency, you will need an agreement with the agency, which specifies exactly what the agency will do and/or provide for you (check with your IRB, they may have samples of such agreements). Include a copy of the agreement in your appendix. Let me go through an example for you. Let us say you want to access the medical records from a nursing home regarding the medications of all patients with Parkinson's disease. You will typically not be permitted by the IRB to go through the patients' charts yourself; instead, you will need a staff member from the nursing home to agree to go through the records and write down all of the needed info without the patients' names. Therefore, the written agreement from the nursing home would state they agree that XX will gather the specified information for you and no names will be included in the final data set.

Next, indicate your approval number and date from the IRB, if you need to get approvals from other IRBs, list them here. Discuss any ethical concerns about recruitment materials and a plan to address them. Some examples might include how you will recruit (such as with a flyer); your consent form; and if you are using children, an assent form (similar to a consent form in simpler language) for them. Then you will need to discuss any ethical concerns related to your data collection, such as people refusing participation, stopping midway, and having any possible adverse reactions to the study. Some things to remember that will help with this section. Participants have the right to stop whenever they want. You do however, have to decide what you will do with their data, will you include it or exclude it? Anytime your participants might have emotional issues arise from your study questions you need to find a way to help them. You are not allowed to counsel them, but you could provide phone numbers/ information on low cost counseling or hotlines. If there is any possibility of participants revealing any personal medical, educational information or illegal activity (e.g., child or elderly abuse, drug use), you must have a plan as to how you will handle it.

Next, you need to describe how you will protect your data. State if the data is considered confidential (you know who provided it) or anonymous (you do not know who provided it). If data are confidential, and it is possible to determine later who provided it, extra protections are required (an example is if there are five women who work at a given agency with 30 men, you will want to disguise them so it is not possible for the reader to identify them). You will want to maintain the data on password protected flash drives or external hard drive and limit access to it. State you will destroy all data after seven years (what APA suggests).

Finally, describe any special ethical considerations for your study, such as doing a study at your workplace, conflict of interest issues, and if you are using incentives, such as gift cards. Incentives are often not recommended (it can be considered a form of coercion). Check with your IRB as to their recommendations. I will go into more detail on the IRB and ethical issues in the next chapter.

Research Ethics

Students are often surprised at the many rules related to the Institutional Review Board (IRB), why are they there? If you have a good understanding of the background, perhaps it will be easier for you to write your Chapter 3 and to go through IRB review.

Let us begin with where many of the rules came from, the National Research Act of 1974, which established the National Commission for Protection of Human Subjects of Biomedical and Behavioral Research. This committee's goal was to develop clear ethical guidelines involving human subjects in research. In 1978, the commission wrote what has come to be known as the Belmont Report (because it was written while the group met at the Belmont Conference Center near Baltimore).

Belmont Principle 1: Respect for Persons

There are two ethical statements related to the principle of respect for persons:

1) Individuals are treated as autonomous agents.
2) Persons with diminished autonomy are given protection.

From these two statements four additional conditions have developed that are requirements for IRB approval of research:

a) Voluntary consent to participate in research
b) Informed consent to participate in research

c) Protection of privacy and confidentiality

d) The right to withdraw from research participation without penalty

Let us unpack all of these ideas; consider the first statement concerning the right to individual autonomy and self-determination. This means each person has the right to make his or her own choices and decisions. The second statement states people with a diminished ability to make decisions must be protected. To whom are they referring? Children are considered to not have full intellectual development and have a protected legal status in the United States, so they must be protected. Similarly, prisoners no longer have the legal right to make many decisions, so they are protected. People who are in situations in which their ability to think clearly has been compromised, are protected. Some examples of this include people in crisis situations, patients, and people with reduced mental capacity due to dementia or other mental disorder. In addition, people who do not have the educational background to understand the implications of being in a research study are considered protected. These protected individuals are often called vulnerable subjects.

Vulnerable Subjects and Coercion. When vulnerable individuals are included in a research proposal, the IRB will require some protections to be put in place to protect them. If the subjects are unable to make a fully informed decision about participating in the study, the IRB may require informed consent from a well-educated and properly motivated surrogate decision maker. Some examples may be parents of children or a family member of a dementia patient. If the possibility of coercion is present, an independent subject advocate may be required for the consent process. An example of this might be a homeless individual with questionable mental health status may need to have a social worker available to advocate for him or her. Even for mentally healthy individuals, if there is specific important information, which must be understood, provisions may be needed to test the subject's understanding. An example of this might be in a drug trial of a new medication, the subjects may be required to show an understanding of possible long-term side effects.

What do I mean by coercion? This means that a person to some degree is forced or at least pushed to do something that they may not really wish to do. Another term for this concept is "undue influence." When people are coerced into participating in a research study, they lose their autonomy or their ability to make their own decisions. The IRB will examine whether there is any possible coercion in how you describe your study. Some things to keep in mind about this concept, people in any authority position (e.g., a boss, supervisor, physician, or teacher) may coerce participation simply by directly asking the person to be in the study. In-person solicitation of participation is generally perceived as more coercive than a written ad or flyer (i.e., it is harder to say no in person).

Consent, Privacy and Confidentiality. What do we mean that a person must give "informed consent" before they can participate in research? What is the big deal? This is actually a fundamental issue of ethical research. It means that subjects understand the implications of their decision to be in the research study, and that they agree to participate. As an extreme example, consider a person who is asked to be in a study of a new drug. Many side effects are not known, but similar drugs are known to cause permanent problems such as tremors and blindness. The subjects considering such participation must understand all implications of being in the study. Okay, I can hear you saying, "But my little study can't cause permanent harm!" How do you know? Let us say, you are asking people about their childhood memories, how do you know you will not trigger something about child or sexual abuse they had forgotten? There are always potential effects of being in a study; you want people to carefully consider their participation.

What happens if you want to do research with people who are not competent to give informed consent, e.g., someone with dementia? Such individuals require additional protections, one possibility is the use of "substituted judgment" which means someone else (e.g., next of kin, facility director) makes the decision based on what they believe the person would want to do in the given situation.

The Belmont Report (1994) defined privacy as "having control over the extent, timing, and circumstances of sharing oneself (physically, behaviorally, or intellectually) with others" (Chapter 3). So this relates to how the information is collected from individuals, who may be present, and where it is done. On the other hand, confidentiality pertains to the treatment of information that an individual has disclosed in a relationship of trust and with the expectation that it will not be divulged to others in ways that are inconsistent with the understanding of the original disclosure without permission (Chapter 3).

Therefore, confidentiality is related to what you do with the information after it is collected. Why is this important? Consider if you are asking about drug or alcohol use and the subject can be identified by their employer. It may be grounds for dismissal. Alternatively, if it is a prisoner, the information may result in a longer incarceration. Even a simple psychological survey, if a name was attached, may result in embarrassment and feeling of stigmatization. It is a relationship of trust to be a researcher; you must protect your subjects.

Right to Withdraw. The final aspect of the Belmont principle of respect for persons is the right of subjects to withdraw from the study without penalty. This aspect is often the most difficult in practice for researchers. Why? Because as researchers, the reason we have gone through all of the IRB process, recruitment and all it entails, is because we want people to complete our study and get their data. You may discover it is difficult to get people to participate in your study (not an unusual occurrence), so to have someone say they want to stop after they started can be very difficult to hear.

What is the experience like? Let me give you an example from a study I did (in person) for my Senior Honor's Thesis in college. I had a very difficult memory test that both college age and people over 65 completed on the computer. It required the subjects to come up with memory strategies to remember short strings of numbers followed by a distractor task (so they could not rehearse them). It was a frustrating study, particularly for the older people. I had several older people get part way through the study and quit. Keep in mind; it is hard to recruit older adults, so that was devastating for me.

What can you do in these situations? All you can do is thank them for coming, and if you are giving any participation gifts, you give that to them and send them on their way. No begging them to stay and no special incentives. Let them leave. It is hard, but you must respect their decision.

If you decide to do a computer survey, realize you are going to lose data, similar to the above, some people will not complete it. You may have even done this yourself when a survey seemed too long and involved; you just close the link. It gives you a little different view when thinking about it as the researcher!

Keep in mind that a basic ethical principle is people have the right to stop their participation at any time without penalty. Their participation is a gift they may choose to take back. Treat them with respect and courtesy, honor the time they have given you.

Belmont Principle 2: Beneficence

The second Belmont principle is Beneficence, which is described in the report as securing the well-being of the research subject. You can think of this as being kind to the subjects, and treating them as you would like to be treated. It is this principle that leads the IRB to evaluate the risks and benefits of your research.

The risks of the research must be justified by the potential benefits to the individual and to society. As an example, a common issue that arises in the IRB is a researcher wants to go into an elementary school and administer a scale to students measuring something unrelated to their schoolwork (e.g., their relationships with their pets). There may be some benefits to society to know about this topic, however, the risks of students missing classwork for a study unrelated to school are too high. The researcher would be told to find another venue to recruit participants.

A final aspect of this principle is that conflicts of interest must be managed so that bias in important judgments related to research conduct is unlikely. An example of this might be an instructor recruiting his or her students. It would be very difficult for students to say no, if asked directly. Other potential conflicts are having some financial interest in the results (for example, doing a study to show that your program, in which you have a financial interest, works). The researcher may consciously or unconsciously influence the results because of their interests in the outcome.

This principle can be best understood as treating the participants as you would like to be treated. Again, as a researcher you have a responsibility to protect those who volunteer for your study.

Belmont Principle 3: Justice

The Belmont principle of Justice is a little trickier to understand. It was developed in response to studies that exploited some of the most vulnerable groups in society, such as the Tuskegee syphilis study and the use of prisoners for drug studies. The easiest way to understand the principle of justice is that your research project should not systematically exclude a specific class or type of person who is likely to benefit from research participation or in whom the results of a specific kind of research are likely to be applied.

What does this mean? It means if the results of your study will be generalized to the general population, then one group of people (e.g., young adults) may not be the only ones participating in the study. An example might be a drug study, if you as the researcher want the drug to be ultimately taken by anyone; then different races, ethnic groups, ages, and genders need to participate in the drug trials.

How does this principle apply to your study? You must have a very good reason for excluding anyone in your study. Carefully think through to whom your study applies and how you will recruit them. Think through the population in your area; is there any way to recruit people of different races?

Chapter 3: Lucy

Recall your future dissertation reader, grad student Lucy, is reading your paper. The key issue for Lucy in reading your Chapter 3, regardless of your methodology, is understanding what you did in the study. It needs to be explained in enough detail that she could replicate it if she wanted. What does this mean for you, as a writer? It means you must clearly define who is eligible to be in your study and how you decided how many people should participate. Thoroughly explain any measures you used, give statistics on the reliability and validity of the measures.

Did you do a pilot study? Why? Explain how you went about it. Discuss exactly how you recruited your participants. What did they see as potential subjects (e.g., ads, flyers, etc.); include them in your appendix. How did they let you know they wanted to participate? What happened when they started the actual study? Was it done in a group? Individually? Online? How did you maintain privacy? How long did it take people to complete the study? Be sure to include all measures, permissions to use them, interview questions, etc. in your appendix. Discuss the ethical issues in your study, how you went about protecting your subjects and their data. Finally describe your plan for analysis of your data.

Why do you have to include all of this? Because Lucy needs to be able to clearly see how your study differs from the one she is considering. She needs to know how your participants are different from her population. Should she use the same measures you used or different ones? How should she structure her methods based upon your study? Think of Chapter 3, in particular, as teaching Lucy about your study. Make sure she clearly understands the rationale for your methods as well as how you went about it.

A Complete Proposal!

You have a draft of the first three chapters, now what? First give yourself a cheer and celebrate, then begin the rewriting process. Rewriting?? Yes, you have done a first draft, hopefully including all of the necessary parts, but it is rough, and needs a lot of polishing. I suggest reading through the draft in full, make notes to yourself (I use track changes) and mark areas that are not complete, may not be clear to someone reading it for the first time, or need more support with citations. Then start at the beginning and read each sentence aloud, is there a way to make it clearer, more concise? Picture your grandmother, who knows nothing about your area of study, reading it: would she understand that sentence? Check for any pronouns (they, he, and she); is it clear to whom the pronouns are referring? Check your plurals versus possessives (this makes me crazy when they are wrong): plurals (e.g. "girls") do not have an apostrophe, possessives do have an apostrophe (e.g., "the girl's bike;" "the girls' bikes"). Do you know a former English major? Someone who is a great writer? If so, ask them to read through your paper and offer suggestions.

As you prepare to send your proposal on to your committee, I would like you to consider how well you accept criticism. No one likes to be criticized, but it is part of life and particularly part of academia. Instead of taking it personally, remember you are a student, is not part of being a student learning new things? Do you want the best paper and project it is possible to have? The only way it will happen is to listen to criticism. Assume for a moment, you have just received an edited draft from your committee member, how do you handle this? I suggest reading through their comments then setting it aside for a few hours to a day. Think about the comments, instead of reacting. When you are calm and ready, start at the beginning and take each comment as a learning experience. Fix it, then look for similar issues in the paper and fix those. Go on to the second comment, etc. I look at comments and suggestions as a challenge, can I fix these and have the person read the paper again and not find any issues? When you are done with your revisions read through the paper one more time (at least) and make sure it reads well.

Do You Feel Like an Imposter?

It is very common for students to feel insecure and that they are simply pretending to be a doctoral student. You may feel that if people really understood how little you know they would not allow you to get a Ph.D.! This feeling actually has a name, the Imposter Syndrome, and it is particularly common in students who are the first in their family to get a doctorate. If you consider it carefully, it makes total sense that you feel this way: you have not known many people socially who have a doctorate and you are, in all likelihood seeing them as smarter than or more creative than you are.

Let us consider if this true. Would you expect a doctoral student to know as much as an accomplished researcher or professor? Of course not, the student is in school to learn. Give the student 20 years and he or she will be as knowledgeable and confident as any other professional is.

You are that doctoral student! You are not expected to know everything at this point. So relax, and take the opportunity to meet other students and doctoral level researchers and get to know them as people. Ask about their families and home lives and you will begin to realize they are similar to other people you know and to you. You have earned your place in your doctoral program; you will gain the necessary experience you need to be successful and graduate!

Moving On: The Proposal Defense

Once your committee has approved your proposal (Chapters 1-3) your institution may have additional steps before you can defend your proposal, some examples are running the paper through plagiarism software, and having other faculty read it. You will then be able to schedule your (typically) one-hour proposal defense. You will need to select several possible days and times that will work for you and send those to your committee (check with your chair first, he or she may like to follow a different procedure).

In advance of the defense, you will want to prepare a power point for your committee. Ask how long you will be allowed to talk, it is often 20-30 minutes, check with your committee as how many slides they think is appropriate. It is better to have just an outline on the slides, you can always write out everything you want to say and go through it during your presentation. Concentrate on the methods and analyses with just enough literature to put it into context. Check with your chair how he or she likes it done. If you are in an online institution, you will probably need to send your committee the power point prior to the defense call.

On the day of the defense, have your computer ready and a copy of your paper available for reference. It is also a good idea to have some water available, if you need it (taking a drink is also a great delaying tactic to give you time to consider a question). Once the meeting starts, your committee will greet you and try to put you at ease, and then it will be your turn to go through the presentation.

A few things to know, first this is typically not a confrontational situation. I know it is called a defense, but it is really just a chance for the committee to hear about the project one more time and catch anything they may have missed. It is typically very collegial, with everyone trying to make it the best project possible. After your 20 minute talk, your committee will ask you questions. They are just trying to clarify any issues that might arise during the data collection. It is okay to say you do not know something (but say you will check it out, find the answer, and report back).

Take a few moments at this stage of the process to reflect on your progress, celebrate! Your next step is the IRB (Institutional Review Board), this is the ethics review and takes place before you collect any data. I will take a look at the IRB process next.

CHAPTER 11
IRB (INSTITUTIONAL REVIEW BOARD)

Once your committee has approved your proposal, next is the Institutional Review Board review (ethics board). The first step is to find your IRB website, and download the IRB application. Often you are required to take a short ethics course online, if so, do that and get it out of the way. When you are done with the course, save the certificate to your computer, you will need to submit it to the IRB.

What is the IRB looking for? They want to know you have thought out every detail of your study. The most common error students make is not providing enough detail, or not being clear in the information provided. As you begin to complete the IRB application, think about each item and consider: will someone unfamiliar with your study understand what you have written? Keep in mind the board typically does not read your proposal, they rely on the information you provide in your application.

The IRB is most concerned with your interactions with your participants, so go into great detail in this area. Think through each aspect of your study, some examples: Who will approach possible participants? What will they say? What happens to participants at each step of the process? Go into excruciating detail. If you find yourself assuming things (e.g., "I'll use a room at XX for the interview") stop and rethink it, do you have permission to use the room? Will it be private? Can people easily get there and find it? Will using the building give the impression the organization is sponsoring the study? An example, of the last question would be using a church; you would want to be clear in your recruitment materials that the church is not affiliated in any way with your study.

It might be helpful for me to work through a fake study and think through some of the issues in the research methods. As an example, I want to look at car shopping decisions and the relationship with the new owner's self-efficacy (self-confidence). My initial plan is to do a mixed method study; I will use a standardized, brief self-efficacy survey and briefly interview the customer (some example questions: What was your decision at the dealership regarding buying a car? What led you to make the decision that you did?). I decide I want to use a local Nissan dealership, so first I approach the general manager, John Smith, and see if there is some way to make this work. John is open to the dealership participating but does not want me to interfere with customers in their decision making process. I initially discuss having everyone who speaks with a salesperson complete the five-question survey. A brief consent form will be included and ask whether a researcher can contact them by phone and ask for their name and phone number. I plan then to call each customer that agrees and ask my questions.

What are issues I need to consider? First, I will need a letter from John Smith stating everything that his people will and will not do, and any information that the dealership will provide to us (I should wait on actually getting the letter from John Smith until I have finalized all of the details of my study; things may still change). Second, I want to make it very clear that the researchers are not affiliated in any way with the dealership, that the person is not required to participate, and no one will treat them differently regardless of their choice in participating. One issue the IRB is going to have is with the salesperson giving out the survey, which gives the appearance of the dealership sponsoring the study. Is there a way around this? Perhaps at the end of the salesperson interaction he or she could give them a flyer with a link to an online survey (and the consent form and request for an interview) on survey monkey (this is an online site where you can construct surveys and collect data)? As a researcher, I need to consider that this is going to lower the participant rate (people may throw away my flyer, they may lose interest in participating, only people with computer access could participate), but it will make it more acceptable to the IRB. As a result, I will probably have to continue the study longer and will need to mention this issue in the limitation section of the paper.

Consider the study's inclusion criteria. People may participate if they are 18 years and older and if they are able to read English, which is the language of the survey. I should ask their age at the beginning of the survey to double check they qualify to participate. The exclusion criteria are being under 18 and unable to read English.

What other demographics might be a factor in purchasing a car? Perhaps marital status, having children, sharing decision-making, employment, income per year. I would want to check the literature, make a decision, and add these into the survey. How will I determine who is interviewed? I will need to preset a rule for this. It could be the first 10 people who agree to be interviewed, or if I think marital status is important I could say the first five with a partner/ spouse and the first five single/ divorced people who volunteer will be selected. The important thing is to select the criteria in advance and stick to it. Here is my current method:

1. Get permission letter from John Smith
2. Prepare flyer for salespeople with a link in survey monkey
3. Prepare survey monkey with a consent form and the the survey. At the end of the survey, ask if person can be contacted for an interview, if they agree, have them give their email or phone number.
4. Have a brief meeting with salespeople explaining the study and that we would like them to give a flyer to every customer, whether they buy a car or not.
5. Wait to see if we get participants
6. Contact those willing to be interviewed
7. Call for interviews, record interviews
8. Transcribe interviews
9. Analyze qualitative data, developing coding
10. Download survey data from survey monkey
11. Analyze survey results compared to qualitative coding
12. Send results to participants and dealership

After a month, I only have three participants! I need to rethink my method, some possible options: I could go to the dealership and hand out the flyer personally as the person is leaving the dealership, sometimes the personal contact will help. I could increase the number of dealerships; each dealership will require that I go through the first four steps listed above. Whatever, my final decision, I will need to notify the IRB I am changing the procedure.

A few final thoughts on the IRB process, you may need to go through several revisions of your methods with the IRB. Work through each of the IRB's comments and think them through. If you cannot figure out a solution, ask for a conference call (or meet in person) with the IRB and your chair and they will brainstorm with you. Again, always be professional in your interactions, they are not trying to delay your progress. They just want your study to be the best one possible that protects you and your participants.

External IRBs

Depending upon your study design, you may need to get permission from other IRBs or organizational gatekeepers. If you are working with another institution, for example a college, prison, military, or hospital you may need to get approval through their IRB too.

If your design includes another institution, begin your discussions early and find out their requirements. Often they will want you to secure your home institution's IRB approval before they review it. However, any guidelines will be helpful to you in understanding the procedures you must follow.

If you are considering working with children, elderly, ill patients, prison, or military populations be aware that these are considered protected populations and special care must be taken. Prisons and the military are often very difficult institutions in which to conduct research, so be prepared for a long battle to secure approvals. A similar dilemma is faced for accessing Native Americans living on reservations through the Bureau of Indian Affairs. Plan ahead for paperwork and dealing with bureaucracies. It often helps to work with a cultural broker or someone familiar with the organization/ culture.

A few tips for approaching such entities, always be professional. It may become very frustrating but keep your cool; they are protecting their populations. There may be a ridiculous amount of redundant paperwork, but carefully fill each form out and submit by the time indicated. This is not a time to show your independence! Keep a record of whom you talk to, the date of the conversation, and what was discussed. Make a copy of all forms, sometimes things get lost. Keep all emails, in case they are needed later. One of the hallmarks of bureaucracies is being shuffled from person to person, so protect yourself with good records.

To Pilot or Not to Pilot?

A question you will need to consider when you are designing your study is whether to pilot the study on some test subjects. My recommendation is yes! Do it! I always pilot test my studies, and the reasoning is simple, I want to know everything works in the way I have visualized, I want to check how long the study takes to complete, and I want to make sure everything is clear to the subject. Be aware, you must have IRB approval before conducting any pilot studies.

Whom should you ask to be pilot subjects? There are a number of schools of thought on this. If there are concerns about the suitability of your questions, you may want to consider selecting people who are familiar with your topic but not necessarily eligible for your study. Let us use an example of a study on women who are currently in domestic violence relationships, I would recommend for a pilot, searching for women who were formerly in such relationships. They would be familiar with the topic but you are not using possible participants. You can then make any needed changes (and submit the changes to IRB), before you test real participants.

I would also recommend using the above procedure if you are using a technique with which you are unfamiliar. Therefore, if you have never conducted a qualitative interview (even if you have done other types of interviews), take the time to do some practice ones. You can get over your nervousness, learn how to pace yourself, and learn the value of being silent and waiting for the participant to think about their response. Plan to always debrief your pilot subjects by speaking to them about your study when you are done with their testing/ interview. Ask them how long it took to complete any surveys and how they felt about it (e.g., bored, annoyed, interested). Ask if any questions were vague or any words unclear. Also, ask if there were things they wished you had asked them (this is always a good last question for any interview).

A second option is to have friends or family members be test subjects. This is best used for general surveys, when anyone is eligible to be in a study. It is not advisable to have someone pretend to fit a specific subgroup (e.g., domestic violence victims). You can use family or friends for trying out the technique, but I do not recommend this for any official pilot interviews; family and friends will not respond in the same way as people you do not know, so you really will not get the experience you need.

A third piloting option (if you have experience in the technique) is to consider having your first few "real" subjects be potential pilot subjects. Again, interview them after they are done and ask about the issues listed above. If no changes are needed, then you can count them as "real" subjects. However, if you need to make any changes in the materials, questions, or your techniques they may not be included in your official sample.

Treat pilot testing seriously, record your interactions with the subject, go back, and listen to the recording. Everyone hates to hear their own voice, but it is particularly important with interviews that you make sure you are giving people sufficient time to answer. New researchers tend to worry about the next questions they will be asking, the trick is to learn to pay attention to the interviewee's response. Did they actually answer your question? Did you cut off their answer? In the next chapter, we will discuss issues related to collecting the data for your study..

CHAPTER 12
DATA COLLECTION

Finally, you have all the approvals and get to collect your data! A few pointers for this phase. Make sure you follow the procedures that were listed in your IRB application exactly; this is also called your research protocol. The IRB may do random audits of researchers' (especially students') data, so be sure you are scrupulous about maintaining your protocol. Any changes (even minor ones) must be approved by the IRB. If you make any major changes, also be sure you notify your committee members, and get their okay on it.

One detail that is rarely mentioned is the need for organizing your data. Let us consider a couple of different scenarios. If you are using any type of paper collection methods (surveys, questionnaires, etc.) keep everything in one place, such as a file folder or large envelopes. Do not throw away or destroy anything until your total dissertation is complete (even if you enter the data into software), you may need to double check your originals and if you are audited by the IRB, you will need the originals.

If you are downloading your data directly from an outside source, e.g., survey monkey or secondary data, be sure you double check that the data makes sense. Sometimes things get messed up in the transfer. Save your data in a couple of places, just in case of computer issues. Always double-check your data entry; it is worth having someone else check you. Your results will only be as accurate as your data entry.

One question students doing qualitative research often have is whether they can deviate from their IRB approved interview questions. You are allowed to ask follow up questions to clarify the participants' responses, but you may not go into new topics. If you believe you need an additional interview question(s), you must notify the IRB, you will also need to show

how the new interview questions relate to your research questions.

If you are interacting directly with your participants through interviews or other methods, keep in mind, these people are doing you a great favor by being in your study. You could not get your degree without them. So be accommodating to their schedule, be polite, and thank them for participating. You have an obligation to all future researchers to show your participants that involvement in research is important and enjoyable.

As you wait for the data to come in, use this time to go back through your proposal and change everything related to your study from future tense ("the study will explore…") to past tense ("the study explored…"). Do not rely on a search and replace, I guarantee you will have to later go back and fix errors. Instead, read through the paper and correct them. You can also save yourself time in the future by double-checking your Dissertation Guidebook as to form and style issues. Make sure you have followed the rules of grammar and writing as closely as possible.

Data Collection Problems and Resolutions

Things happen in the real world when you are conducting a study, as the researcher it is your responsibility to both recognize the issue and resolve it. Here are some of the most common issues that may arise.

Confidentiality breach. Imagine you are doing a program evaluation. You will survey participants before the program begins and again after the program. In order to match each person's pre and post program survey, you will have them write their names on each form. Somehow, during the data collection a few surveys are left behind. This is a breach of confidentiality. Someone else could see the responses and know who wrote them. In a program setting, that may not seem a serious offense, but consider if it was one's supervisor who saw a derogatory comment about him or herself.

What to do? First, as soon as the loss is realized, get the surveys back in your possession. Second, report the breach to your committee and the IRB. They may want you to notify the individuals involved, but let them make the decision. You also may want to consider not using names in studies, instead ask people to pick a number or phrase that they will enter on the pre survey and remember for the post survey. A couple of good suggestions are the last four digits of their phone number and their birthdate, if possible setting up the study to be anonymous (neither you nor anyone else knows who participated) would be the best possible solution. In the example above, one solution might be doing the study online (e.g., through survey monkey), which allows the results to be anonymous.

Questionable data. When you are collecting in-person data, you may have someone act strangely, making you suspect drugs or alcohol use. Another scenario is that someone hands in a "completed" survey in a few minutes, as compared to the 20 minutes others took.

What to do? First, make sure you are safe in the case of strange behavior (I once had a participant break the chair in which he was sitting from rocking and bouncing the chair due to amphetamine use). If there are any concerns, thank them for coming and get them out the door quietly. Second, mark their data forms, with the behavior that concerns you. Later when you analyze data, check whether their data deviates from the norm. Discuss the issue with your committee and make a joint decision about whether to include the data in the analyses.

Participant Withdrawal. Occasionally you may have participants indicate they want to stop and do not want to continue in your study. This is most common with special populations, such as the elderly and ill.

What to do? First, I suggest asking if a break might help (and if you can recognize the need for one early, all the better). Second, as frustrating as it may be to lose their data; you should just thank them for coming and let them go.

Incomplete data. Thus far, I have been addressing in-person research concerns, but one that is very common with online data collection is participants skipping questions. Some standardized surveys are invalid if questions are skipped.

What to do? In person, you can do a quick check to see if any data is missing. Online is trickier. Most survey programs (like survey monkey) allow the option for requiring answers to the questions. There are some positives and negatives to consider with this. The positive is your data will be complete, with no missing responses. The negative is some people will quit the survey if they cannot skip responses. An option for demographic questions, is to provide a "choose not to respond" choice, which keeps people in the study, at least through the demographic questions.

Inappropriate disclosure. In interviews, you may have someone tell you things, which are inappropriate, such scenarios include child or elder abuse, and disclosing medical or education information.

What to do? As soon as you realize where they are going, stop them. Say that this is information you should not be told and move on with the study. The exception is if you are a mandated reporter (check the laws in your state, some states say that everyone is a mandated reporter for child or elder abuse). In this case, you are ethically required to report the incident to the appropriate authorities. I suggest first consulting with your committee and the IRB. Your status as a mandated reporter must be disclosed in the consent form. Such disclosures are unusual, but you need to be prepared in case they do happen. Whenever you run into something unexpected, know that you can contact your committee and/ or the IRB for help.

Secondary or Archival Data

What is secondary data? It is data that has already been collected by someone else. It may be data that is collected as a standard practice in an organization (e.g., medical charts, pre-employment testing). Some things to know about this type of secondary data, particularly if it is from an organization where you are employed. First, you will only be able to use information that is available to any outside researcher (you are not allowed to get special treatment as an "insider"). Second, the data will need to be "de-identified" before you get access to it. This means someone else will have to remove all names and identifying information of individuals, so the data is anonymous when you receive it. Check with the IRB early in the process, if you are interested in this option.

Another source of secondary data is large archival datasets that have been made available by the original researchers. Many educational institutions provide students with the opportunity to access datasets. The original researchers provide information on the background, variables, and any coding they used for data input. The use of such a dataset is perfectly acceptable as a dissertation, however a few cautions. Make sure that the study you are considering has not been previously published with the data. Typically, the researchers give a bibliography of all articles published by them. However, it does not mean other people have not published using the data. Search the library carefully, and include dissertations in the search. Use the name of the dataset as a search term. Another very important caution is to do not try to access the data until you have IRB approval, you must have their ok to proceed. Also, be aware it can be tricky to convert the data to SPSS or other statistical software and to understand the logic of their data entry. You probably will not be able to contact the researchers, so you will need to figure it out with the help of your committee.

Archival data analysis is a great way to get access to difficult populations' data; an example might be sex offenders. However, you are stuck with the variables the original researchers used, and there is no possibility of getting additional information from the participants. If you decide to go this route, you can reduce your time to completion considerably, but be prepared to work through the issues I discussed.

Survey Research

Surveys are popular, because they are efficient; researchers can gather a great deal of information for a small cost and generally in a short amount of

time. To consider whether surveys are a good idea for your study, consider these issues (from Vogt, Gardner & Haeffele (2012).
1. The data are best obtained directly from the respondents
2. Your data can be obtained by brief answers to structured questions.
3. You can expect respondents to give you reliable information.
4. You know how you will use the answers.
5. You can expect an adequate response rate.

Now let us consider each of these issues.

1. The data are best obtained directly from the respondents.
Often the only way to obtain information about people is by asking them. This is especially true of subjective data, i.e., the inner states of the subjects being studied, such as attitudes, beliefs, or values. You can also use surveys to collect objective data, such as respondents' age, income, or years of work experience, which could be obtained in other ways, but it is usually easier simply to ask. However, if you have access to records, such as educational and medical records, these may be more accurate and possibly more efficient than asking individuals. People's memories are notoriously poor on such questions, as "how often have you visited your doctor in the past year." Having access to their records would make it much more accurate. Keep in mind that asking unimportant or needless questions tend to annoy participants and they may quit your study because of it.

2. Your data can be obtained by brief answers to structured questions.
Surveys work best when asking structured questions. Structure refers to the degree of control you want to exercise over the answers you will get. The questions may be either completely unstructured and vague or highly structured. The more structured the questions, the more participants are constrained to your predetermined answers. Therefore, you may be limiting their responses; they may have other things to say. On the other hand, having broad and exploratory questions as in interviews, may not be the best choice for surveys, as the data may not be able to be summarized.

3. You can expect respondents to give you reliable information.
Sometimes surveys are an unwise choice because respondents may find it difficult to answer accurately or truthfully. Perhaps the information you seek is hard to remember or too sensitive for people to be willing to reveal it to a stranger. It is often assumed that social desirability biases much survey research, meaning that respondents may answer questions to reflect what they think is socially appropriate rather than what they really believe or do. Racial beliefs and attitudes provide an example of this. An example given by Vogt et al. (2012) is in the second half of the 20th century, the

number of people answering national surveys in ways indicating they held a racial prejudice dropped rapidly compared to earlier surveys. Whether people were less prejudiced in the 1990s than in the 1950s is uncertain. However, it is clear that the behavior of respondents on the same survey questions dramatically changed.

4. You know how you will use the answers.

You need to have a clear idea as to how you will use the survey questions to address your research questions. Keep in mind that short surveys are generally much better than long ones in keeping participants focused and finishing the survey.

Each of your research questions typically relate to a number of survey questions. It is a good idea to match up your research and interview questions to make sure that you will actually be able to answer your research questions. If you have survey questions without a matching research question, you probably do not need the survey questions. If you have a research question without a survey question, you need to add more survey questions. Here is an example of matching a research question and survey questions.

Research Questions	Survey Questions
1. How do patients' searches, for health related information on the internet, relate to visits to their primary health provider?	1. In the past month, have you searched for health related information on the internet? 2. Before your most recent visit to your primary health provider, did you search for any health related information on the internet? 3. After your most recent visit to your primary health provider, did you search for any health related information on the internet?

You should also have a plan as to how you will analyze the data you collect. Without such a plan, you may come to realize that you have collected hundreds of surveys with a missing variable that is needed for your analysis. As an example, if you would like to analyze your data using gender as an independent variable, make sure you have included it in the survey.

5. You can expect an adequate response rate.

An otherwise excellent survey study can be ruined by a low response rate. The difficulty is that if only a small proportion of the people you ask to be in the survey actually complete it, you can no longer generalize to the population of interest. For this reason, if you suspect a low response rate is likely, you would be better off having fewer people and then interview them.

What is a good response rate? There is not a clear answer to this. You will need to review the literature and see what others report. There are a few things you can do to improve your response rate. Using a university's participant pool, generally results in a high rate of response (keep in mind they are not representative of the general population). If you can guarantee respondents that their answers will be anonymous (the researcher does not know who responded), it generally helps. The second best choice is guaranteeing confidentiality (only the researcher knows who responded).

What Mode for Your Survey?

There are three modes of administering surveys, they are face-to-face, telephone, and self-administered (on paper or through the computer). How do you decide which to use? There is no single best method; all have advantages and disadvantages, which are summarized in the table below (modified from Vogt et al., 2012, p. 20).

Mode of administration

Advantages and disadvantages	Face-to-Face	Telephone	Self-Administered
1. Usable with respondents who cannot read	Yes	Yes	No
2. Researcher can explain the meaning of a question	Yes	Yes	No
3. Researcher knows identity of respondent	Yes	Yes	No
4. Interaction with administer of survey	High	Medium	Low
5. Certainty that all respondents get exactly the same question	Low	Medium	High
6. Cost per respondent	High	Medium	Low
7. Time per question	High	High	Low
8. Possible to administer in groups	Yes	No	Yes
9. Effort required to obtain a large sample size	High	Medium	Low
10. Problems of access to respondents in remote or unsafe areas	Yes	No	No

11. Researcher's efficiency tied to that of postal, internet, or telephone system	No	Yes	Yes

As the researcher, you need to weigh each of these considerations, keeping both the advantages and disadvantages in mind.

Resisting Temptation

You have started your study, but you are not getting many participants. A small little voice in your head suggests it would be so easy to make up the data… no one would know… When that voice starts whispering to you, hear my voice shouting, "DON'T DO IT!" There are many ramifications of falsifying data, let us begin with a recent story in the news. Donald Green, a researcher at Columbia University and Michael LaCour, published a study last December in the journal Science. In the study, Green and LaCour reported results that suggested voters' support for same-sex marriage increases following a 20-minute conversation with a gay advocate for same-sex marriage.

Intriguing results, are they not? Other researchers attempted to replicate the results. When they were unable to do so, they contacted the original researchers and the journal and wanted to know more about the original data. Green could not produce his data, as more questions were asked; it was found he lied about funding sources also.

What are the implications of your making up data? You can have your Ph.D. revoked, be dismissed from the university (with no ability to return), if you received any grant funding you could face criminal charges for fraud. In addition, your professional career is finished before you started. You would never be able to use anyone from your institution as a reference, as a result getting a job or entering another program would be difficult to impossible.

Recently IRBs have begun randomly auditing data (particularly collected from students). Falsifying data is not worth it. As a professional, you have a responsibility to be ethical in all aspects of your study. If you are having problems getting enough participants, talk to your committee. If your data is not coming out as expected, talk to your committee. There are ethical solutions, let the experienced researchers guide you to them.

Interviewing

I have been repeatedly asked by students to talk more about interviewing. I will be using as the basis for this section Seidman's (2012) book on interviewing. So why do interviews? Interviewing is hearing people's stories and understanding the meaning of their behavior and how they see the world.

The purpose of interviewing is not to test a hypothesis or to evaluate, rather it is to discover the lived experience of people and to understand the meaning they give the experience. Therefore, this means listening to people and as an interviewer realizing you are not having a mutual discussion; instead, you are listening to what the participant has to say. You need to show you are valuing their opinion and not leading them to respond in a way that serves your own agenda.

Phrasing your research question becomes very important; you must not have a predetermined outcome in mind. Thus, if you are interested in the experience of online students in writing a dissertation, you do not want to ask: "Do online dissertation students hate working in an online environment?" You are predicting an outcome. Instead, a more general question is better: "What is the lived experience of being an online dissertation student?"

Why Not To Do Interviews

Time: interviews take a great deal of time to plan, interview, transcribe, and analyze the data. Doing a qualitative study is not the "easy way" to do research. Transcription of interviews takes hours and there really is not a fast and easy way to do it (unless you can afford to have someone else do it).

Being shy: doing interviews requires you to recruit and contact people you do not know. If you are very shy or afraid to contact strangers, the process can be insurmountable.

Not understanding other methodologies: often students decide on qualitative methods and fail to really understand quantitative methods (or vice versa). This is very limiting in the end; it may mean that you have limited future job opportunities. Make sure that you get as much experience as you can in all methods, so your options remain open.

Ethical/moral issues: there may be ethical reasons for not interviewing certain people/ populations as it may be exploitative and potentially damaging to them. An example would be interviewing illegal immigrants or prisoners, who could potentially be hurt if their comments were identified as coming from particular individuals. Interviewing needs to be carefully considered as a research method and needs to be a fit for your personality, time, and your population.

Phenomenological Interviewing: Philosophy

Phenomenology is actually a philosophical approach to interviewing. Different researchers have slightly different methods and views for what they call phenomenology, I will be talking about the view set forth by Seidman (2012). Phenomenology is examining the experience of participants and the meaning they make of it; this view stresses the transitory nature of human experience. As Seidman states (p. 16) "in human experience, the 'will be' becomes the 'is' and then the 'was' in an instant." Therefore as interviewers, we are interested in the participant's "is," recognizing that it may change in the future.

Consider in most of life we are seeing the world from our point of view, which may be quite different from how others view it. In phenomenological interviewing, the goal, as the researcher, is to set our own beliefs about the world aside and understand the world from the interviewee's viewpoint. We will never fully understand their view, but we must strive to come as close as we can.

Researchers emphasize that a phenomenological approach focuses on the "lived experience" of others. What does "lived experience" mean? It means both the interviewer and interviewee step back and reflect on the reconstruction of what the interviewee felt during the phenomenon of interest. Interviewers strive to guide the interviewee to recreate mentally their lived experience, trying to make the "was" into the "is."

Finally, a phenomenological approach emphasizes the meaning of experiences. A basic assumption is that the meaning people make of their experience affects how they live the experience. By asking participants to reconstruct their experience and reflect on it, researchers are asking people to give meaning to it. It is the context of the experience: their feelings, rationale, and thoughts about the experience, which gives it meaning. Therefore, understanding the person's words that he or she chooses to use become very important; clarity of meaning is the goal. As an interviewer, you must put the experience into the wider context of the person's life. For example, knowing a woman is currently a dissertation student only can be understood when you understand what it means to her in the context of her life.

A Three Interview Series

Phenomenological interviewing requires an understanding of both the context and the meaning a participant associates with a particular phenomenon. Seidman (2012) recommends the use of a three-interview series, in order to delve deeply in the context and to establish trust with the participant. Interview 1 establishes the context of the participant's experience. Interview 2 allows the participant to reconstruct the details of their experience within the context in which it occurred. Interview 3 encourages the participant to reflect on the meaning of the experience. While, interviewing your subjects three times may not be possible, you can still approach a single interview by bringing in characteristics of the three-interview series detailed here.

Interview One: Focused Life History. In the first interview, the interviewer's task is to put the participant's experience into context by talking about him or herself in light of the topic of interest. The interviewer avoids the use of "why" questions, using "how" questions instead. For example, "how did you come to be in an online dissertation program?" By asking "how" you are leading the person to reconstruct the event and place it into the context of their family, school, and work experience.

Interview Two: The Detail of Experience. The second interview concentrates on the details of the participant's current life in the topic area. Here you are collecting details upon which their later opinions will be built. As an example, you might ask online dissertation students what they do each day related to their dissertation. You are trying to get the person to reconstruct the many details of his or her life that make up the experience of interest. Thus, you might ask about the dissertation student's relationships with his or her chair, committee member, other students, spouse or partner, children, work colleagues, and friends. You might ask them to reconstruct a day in their dissertation life from the moment they woke up until they fell asleep. You may ask for stories about their experiences in school as a way to of eliciting details.

Interview Three: Reflection on Meaning. In the third interview, participants are asked to reflect on the meaning of their experience. It addresses the intellectual and emotional connections between the participant's work and life. An example question with an online dissertation student might be: "Given what you have said about life before you started your dissertation and what you said about your dissertation work now, what does completing a dissertation mean to you in your life?" Making sense or meaning requires that the participant look at how the factors in his or her life interacted to bring him or her to the present situation.

Bias in Qualitative Studies

Jane asks: "how do you avoid bias in qualitative interviewing and analysis of data?

Great question, Jane! There are some safeguards built into the process, if you follow the standard qualitative protocols (e.g., see Creswell & Plano, 2011). Here are some general guidelines. First, make sure your research questions are neutral, so you are not predicting a particular outcome. For example, "What is the experience of homeless people in dealing with the medical community?" is more neutral and less biased than "Do homeless people believe the medical community is dangerous?"

Second, when you write your interview questions, remember they must follow from your research questions, be open-ended, and they must be neutral. You should not lead the participant into a particular belief you have about them, instead you want the participant to say or indicate whether the issue is important. An example would be, "tell me about your last medical visit." This is much more neutral and more likely to get you their opinions than "do you think all doctors are ageist?"

The third way to reduce your bias is to keep a journal (or field notes) where you write down your opinions and insights. Here is where you get a chance to note your biases and internal beliefs. Do not express them to your participants.

Fourth, when analyzing data it is always a good idea to have a second independent person go through and code your data, or at least double-check your coding of responses. This is not a job for a spouse or close family member, instead consider a dissertation peer. If you do not know anyone, check if your committee can suggest a student. You want the independent coder to not know how you are expecting the data to come out, keep them neutral so they can spot any biases you have introduced.

Easy Interview Subjects

As a beginning interviewer, you may want to find the easiest way to recruit potential subjects. Students often want to select people with whom they already have relationship, such as: family, friends, coworkers, students they know, or others they may know. While it is understandable to want to use people you know, it is problematic and complicates, and even contaminates, your interviews.

Family and Friends

Sometimes it is tempting to use family or friends as participants in the study; however, this carries with it some serious issues. First, your prior relationship influences the comfort level they have with you, as the interviewer. Thus, they may be more likely to reveal things to you other people would not, providing a false picture of your sample. Similarly, they may be uncomfortable answering personal questions others would answer (picture asking your grandmother about her sex life, not very comfortable for you or her!).

The other issue with friends and family is you may assume you know what they are talking about and not explore in the depth needed in a research interview. It is a good rule that you do not personally know your subjects.

People You Supervise

Conflicts of interest occur when you interview people you supervise. An example might be a principal interviewing the teachers she/he supervises. However, in the situation of interviewing supervisees, you are placing them in a difficult position. They cannot risk be totally honest with you, if you are also in a position to affect their job. It is advisable to seek similar individuals you do not supervise.

As you can see, there is no easy way to recruit participants. Do not fall for the trap of thinking you can "cheat the system," you will only waste your and your participants' time in conducting unethical research.

Recruiting Interview Subjects

Previously, I discussed you should not recruit people you know for interviews, so how do you recruit people you do not know? There are two common ways, which are typically approved by the IRB:

1) Work through an organization. You can work through an organization to access their employees/ members/ customers/ or patients. Typically, the IRB does not want you to contact personally potential interviewees, instead having the organization forward an email with a description of your study information often works. Alternatively, posting flyers or having handouts available onsite is an option. You will need the organization's permission through a letter of agreement.

2) You may be able to use a snowball recruiting technique in which you give out flyers/ send out a description by email of your study to people you know. You then ask them to forward on the information to people they know. Remember, you should not know your final interviewees. In the next chapter, we will move on to analyze the quantitative data you have collected.

CHAPTER 13
ANALYTIC STRATEGIES: QUANTITATIVE

You collected your quantitative data, now comes the fun part: finding out how your study came out! I will start the discussion of analytic strategies with the basics of quantitative data cleaning and analysis. Start by thinking about how data gets into your SPSS or other statistical software program, there are several options. The first option is to use Survey Monkey or other surveying software sites. They allow you to directly download your data into an SPSS file. You will need to double check everything is as you expect, but in general, the data do tend to be accurate.

The second option is the old-fashioned way of entering the data by hand. This is commonly used when you have used paper surveys/instruments. The concern for this method is it is easy to mistype and introduce errors into your data set. It is a good idea to have someone check your work when entering data. I also recommend doing some descriptive statistics, looking at the range of the scores for each variable to make sure they are as expected (e.g., if you are expecting scores ranging between 1-5 a 55 tells you have entered a wrong number).

What do I mean by data cleaning? There are many definitions, but I am talking about a two-step process. First, double-check all cells are filled, you will probably discover some are not and decisions will need to be made on this. The second step is carefully checking the statistical assumptions of your variables and looking for extreme scores.

Why are these steps necessary? Because the results of your study will only be as accurate as the data you analyze. Therefore, it is very important to take the time to check your data carefully, so you know your results are valid and accurate. I want to refer you to a great book that much of my advice over the next few topics will be based: Osborn's (2013) *Best Practices in Data Cleaning.*

Making Data Make Sense: Missing Data

In almost any research study, there will be missing or incomplete data. Missing data can happen for a number of reasons: participants fail to respond to questions, subjects withdraw or quit studies before they are completed, and data entry errors.

The problem with missing data is nearly all statistical techniques assume or require complete data. There can be legitimately missing data; an example might be a survey in which a person is asked if he or she is married, and if so how long. If you are not married, then you would be correct in leaving the "how long" portion of the question blank.

It is also important to realize legitimately missing data can be meaningful. The missing data allows a validity check and may inform the status of an individual. Osborn (2013) provides a great example. In cleaning the data from an adolescent health risk survey, he noticed some individuals indicated on one question they had never used illegal drugs, but later in the survey when asked how many times they used marijuana, indicated an answer greater than 0. Therefore, an answer they should have skipped (or be missing), showed an unexpected number. The author suggests several possible explanations, such as the subject was not paying attention and answered in error. However, a more intriguing possibility is some subjects did not view marijuana as an illegal drug, which is an interesting possibility that could be examined in future research.

One way of dealing with legitimately missing data is making the missing and present data two separate groups. Using the marriage survey example, we could eliminate non-married individuals from a specific analysis when looking at issues related to being married vs. not married. So instead of asking the silly research question, "How long, on average, do all people, even unmarried people, stay married;" we can ask two more refined questions: "What are the predictors of whether someone is currently married?" and "Of those who are currently married, how long on average have they been married?"

Categories of Missing Data

There are two categories of missing data: data missing at random and data missing not at random. If data are missing randomly, we can assume that they will not bias not the results. However, data missing not at random may be a strong biasing influence.

Let us use an example from Osborn (2013), of an employee satisfaction survey given to schoolteachers. The teachers are surveyed twice, once in September and once in June. Missing random data would mean data missing in June had no relationship to any variable from the September survey (such as satisfaction in Sept., age, and years of teaching). An example, might be if we randomly selected 50% of the people who responded in September to again complete the survey in June, we would legitimately be missing half of the data in June (the 50% of people we did not ask). The missing data would be random and not related to a specific variable such as satisfaction, age, years teaching.

On the other hand, suppose only teachers who were satisfied responded to the survey in June (i.e., people who were dissatisfied were less likely to respond to the survey). Then the missing data are considered missing not at random and may substantially bias the results. Thus, the June survey would show a higher than expected satisfaction score (because unsatisfied people did not participate).

Dealing with Missing Data

How can you deal with missing data? SPSS offers pairwise deletion, which means only those cases with complete data are included in the analysis. If you have few missing data and they are a result of randomness, then such a plan may be acceptable. However, if they are not randomly missing, you could introduce biases.

A second commonly used method is substituting the overall sample's mean for the missing data. The logic of this is that in absence of any other information, the sample's mean is the best representation of an individual's score. If only a few scores are missing, then this may be an acceptable alternative. However, keep in mind the more scores that are replaced, the more you are biasing the sample to the mean.

A third alternative is given by Osborne (2000, 2013) in which a prediction equation is developed through multiple regression. If you have quite a few missing scores, you may want to explore this alternative.

Missing Data as a Variable/ Best Practices

You may wish to examine missing data as an outcome itself, as there may be information in the missing-ness. The act of failing to respond vs. responding might be of interest. This can be examined through a "dummy variable," a new variable you create representing whether a person has missing data or not on a particular variable. You can then do some analyses to see if there are any relationships that develop.

Osborne (2013) provides some best practices in dealing with missing data, which are great to remember.

• First, do no harm; be careful in your methodology to minimize missing data.

• Be transparent. Report any incidence of missing data (rates by variable, and reason for missing data if known). This can be important information for readers.

• Explicitly discuss whether data are missing at random (i.e., if there are differences between individuals with complete and incomplete data).

• Discuss how you, as the researcher, dealt with the issue of incomplete data.

Making Data Make Sense: Extreme Scores

What are extreme scores? They are scores far outside the norm for a variable or population, leading to the conclusion they are not part of your true population and probably do not belong in your analyses. A common operational definition for extreme scores is +/-3 standard deviations (SDs) from the mean.

Recall the standard normal distribution of a population has 68.26% of the population between +1 and -1 SD of the mean (see diagram: [34.13% between 0 to +1 SD] + [34.13% between 0 and -1 SD] = 68.26%).

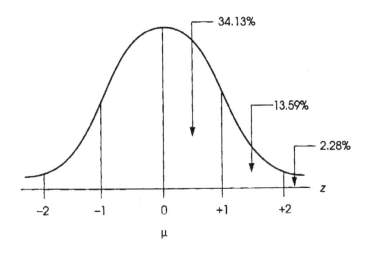

So 95.44% of the population should fall between ±2 SD from the mean (34.13% + 34.13% + 13.59% +13.59% = 95.44%), and 99.74% of the population should fall within ±3 SD of the mean. In other words, the probability of randomly sampling an individual more than ±3 SD from the mean in a normally distributed population is 0.26% (.0026), which gives good justification for considering scores outside ±3 SD as suspect. The concern is these extreme scores are not part of the population of interest in your study.

Extreme Scores Effects and Causes

Extreme scores can cause serious problems for statistical analyses. They generally increase error variance and reduce the power of statistical tests by altering the skew (symmetry of the distribution) or kurtosis (the "peakedness" or flatness of a distribution) of a variable. This can be a problem with multivariate analyses. The more error variance in your analyses, the less likely you are to find a statistically significant result when you should find one (increasing the probability of a Type II error).

Extreme scores also bias estimates such as the mean and SD. Since extreme scores bias your results, you may be more likely to draw incorrect conclusions, and your results will not be replicable and generalizable.

Extreme scores can result from a number of factors. It is possible the extreme score is correct, an example is although the average American male is around 5' 10" there are males who are 7' tall and some who are 4' tall. These are legitimate scores even though they are extreme.

Another cause of an extreme score is data entry error, someone who was actually 5' 8" tall may be incorrectly entered as 8' 5". Therefore, the first step is to always double check the extreme scores were entered correctly. A third cause may be that participants purposefully report incorrect scores. It can also happen that a participant accidently reports an incorrect score. Thus, an extreme score that was entered correctly may need to be evaluated as to whether it should be removed.

Quantitative Analyses

You have collected all of your quantitative data, entered it into SPSS or other statistical software (or downloaded it), and double-checked your data entry. Great... now what?? It can feel intimidating to view your first real data set and know you need to figure out what to do with it. I like to get started with an overall feel for what is going on by calculating means and frequencies. Let us take a moment and review what to use when.

If your variable is continuous, meaning there are no categories you set up previous to the study, you can calculate means and standard deviations. An example of a continuous variable would be where you asked people to enter their age today (e.g., 32, 56, etc.). Examples of categories would be gender: 1 = female, 2 = male or age: 1 = 20-30, 2 = 30-40, etc. Hopefully, these terms are sounding familiar, if not go back to your statistics book and review. A good reference for SPSS is Pallant (2013).

For categorical variables (e.g., gender, education level), you can do a frequency table and get a feel for how your data look. Make sure you do not have any data entry errors, they will show up as a weird number, e.g., you have gender coded as 1 & 2 and 21 shows up in the frequency table. Go back to the original data and double-check it.

One issue you may need to consider is what to do with missing data, for example from people skipping questions. There are a number of ways to deal with this issue (see my previous discussion). Check with your committee to see what they prefer. They will probably ask you how many cells (individual data points) are missing, for which variables are they missing, and what is the largest number missing per individual, so be prepared for those questions.

Once missing data issues are resolved, my usual next step is to run correlations between my variables just to get a feel for what is going on. I then do scatterplots for any that show up as significant. Again, I am just trying to get a feel for the data. My old undergrad statistics professor used to say you need to "take a bath in your data." I like that visual; you need to understand the relationships before being immersed in the formal data analysis.

You should have developed an analysis plan in your proposal, so now is the time to go to it. What happens if you just cannot figure things out? Contact your committee members and ask for help. As a committee member, I sometimes have students send me their data set and I play with it a little, then I can talk them through issues.

Sometimes students decide to hire statistical consultants. Personally, I am not a fan of this. I prefer the student figure out the statistics with the help of his or her committee. The problem with a consultant is you may not really understand what they did and why. Even if they explain it, you really may not have the level of understanding you should. It misrepresents your knowledge level. People reading your dissertation will assume you did the analyses and are capable of doing it (and perhaps teaching it!) again. If you must use a statistics consultant, my advice is to rerun all of the analyses they do, so you understand them too.

Another aspect to consider is keeping track of all the analyses you run and what they show. There are several ways to do this. You can simply save all of your SPSS outputs in a separate file on your computer; if you do this, rename the file with what is in the analysis, e.g., "ANOVA gender & age" (otherwise you have to reopen each file to see it). Another way is to print out all of your data outputs and save them in a file or binder. My own favorite way to keep my data output is to copy it or rewrite it as I go into a Word file. The advantage of this is I am keeping everything together, which is relevant (you will generate a lot of irrelevant information as you go). Do keep in mind that SPSS tables are not in APA format, so any you want to use in your paper will need to be reformatted.

I also find it helpful to think through what I am finding with each analysis (even though this technically goes in Chapter 5, I find it helpful to think about it at the analysis stage). Let us work through an example; I find that my independent variable education level is correlated with my dependent variable, emotional intelligence (EI) total score. So my first question is which education level has a higher EI score? I could do a scatterplot or could just calculate the means for each education level (use Analyze/ Descriptive Stats/ Explore). I then find that people with a graduate degree have a higher emotional intelligence score than people with a high school diploma in the sample. Is this what previous research has found? What if this is not the relationship other researchers have reported? I need to consider why my sample may be different. I check what else is correlated with education, perhaps I find for this sample, gender is highly related to emotional intelligence. Do another scatterplot or Explore between gender and education. Whoa, all of the graduate level participants are female. Could that be the reason education and emotional intelligence score are correlated? Remember your committee can help with any issues you may find. Next, I will do a review of some of the most common statistical tests, how to analyze, and interpret them in SPSS. A great resource for SPSS I recommend is Pallant (2013).

Common Statistical Tests: Analysis and Interpretation
A Quick Reminder of Statistical Terms

If your statistical test results in a $p < .05$, then it is considered statistically significant, and you reject the null hypothesis. If your test results in a $p > .05$, then it is nonsignificant and you retain (NEVER say "accept" the null) the null hypothesis. Generally, a two-tailed test is considered better; because it is a more rigorous test (the p value needed to reject the null is smaller).

One Sample t-tests

You use this test when you are comparing a sample against a known number; an example might be the known population mean on an IQ test. Our research question is: is the sample significantly different from the population mean ($\mu = 100$) for the IQ test? Our null hypothesis is there will be no difference between the sample mean and the population mean of 100. Let us do an example together. Open SPSS and enter the following data for your sample:

115
120
125
130
146

Go to *Analyze/ Compare Means/ One sample t-test*. Move your variable into *Test Variable*. Make your *Test Variable* 100 (mean of the normed IQ test). Press *ok*.

Your results should look like the following:

One-Sample Statistics

	N	Mean	Std. Deviation	Std. Error Mean
VAR00001	5	127.2000	11.90378	5.32353

One-Sample Test

	Test Value = 100					
	t	df	Sig. (2-tailed)	Mean Difference	95% Confidence Interval of the Difference	
					Lower	Upper
VAR00001	5.109	4	.007	27.20000	12.4195	41.9805

What does this mean? Your sample mean is significantly different from the IQ test's population mean of 100. So let us write it up as you would in your paper:

A one-sample t-test was conducted comparing the sample ($M = 127.2$; $SD = 11.9$) to the population mean for the test ($\mu = 100$). The result ($t(4) = 5.109$, $p = .007$) indicates the difference is significant and the null hypothesis is rejected.

What happens if the results were NOT significantly different, as in this example:

102
95
97
103
105

A one-sample t-test was conducted comparing the sample ($M = 100.4$; $SD = 4.22$) to the population mean for the test ($\mu = 100$). The result ($t(4) = .212$, $p = .842$) indicates there is not a significant difference between the two means and the null hypothesis is retained.

Independent Sample t-tests

This statistical test examines whether the means of two separate samples are significantly different. An example might be a control group vs. an experimental group. In this example, the independent variable is condition (control, experimental), the dependent variable is the scores on a test. Our research question is: is the mean for the control group's test scores significantly different from the experimental group's mean? Our null hypothesis is there will be no difference between the two groups. Let us do

Lee Stadtlander, Ph.D.

an example together. So open SPSS and enter the following data for your samples:

Under Variable view (see tab at bottom of page), It should look like:

Name	Type	Width	Decimals	Label	Values	Ignore the rest
condition	numeric	8	0	Condition	*(see below)	Ignore the rest
score	numeric	8	0	Score	None	Ignore the rest

*For condition, labels: 1= control; 2 = experimental

Go back to Data View and enter the following:

Condition	Score
1	5
1	6
1	8
1	2
1	4
2	11
2	15
2	9
2	7
2	12

Go to *Analyze/ Compare Means/ Independent samples t-test*. Move your score variable into *Test Variable*. Move *condition* into *Grouping Variable/ Define groups* 1 and 2. Press ok.

Your results should look like the following:

Group Statistics

	condition	N	Mean	Std. Deviation	Std. Error Mean
score	control	5	5.00	2.236	1.000
	experimental	5	10.80	3.033	1.356

Independent Samples Test

	Levene's Test for Equality of Variances		t-test for Equality of Means							
	F	Sig.	t	df	Sig. (2-tailed)	Mean Difference	Std. Error Difference	95% Confidence Interval of the Difference		
								Lower	Upper
Equal variances assumed	.433	.529	-3.442	8	.009	-5.800	1.685	-9.686	-1.914
Equal variances not assumed			-3.442	7.356	.010	-5.800	1.685	-9.746	-1.854

What does this mean? Your two samples are significantly different from each other (see Sig. column). Let us write it up as you would in your paper:

An independent sample t-test was conducted comparing the control group (M = 5; SD = 2.24) to the experimental group (M = 10.8; SD = 3.03). The result ($t(8)$ =3.4, p= .01) indicates there is a significant difference between the groups and the null hypothesis is rejected.

What happens if the results were NOT significantly different, as in this example:

Condition	Score
1	5
1	6
1	8
1	2
1	4
2	6
2	4
2	7
2	5
2	6

An independent sample t-test was conducted comparing the control group (M = 5; SD = 2.24) to the experimental group (M = 5.6; SD = 1.14). The result ($t(8)$ =-.54, p= .608) indicates there is not a significant difference between the groups and the null hypothesis is retained.

Paired t-tests

A paired sample t-test examines whether the means of one sample tested at two different times are significantly different. An example might be a pre-study survey and post-study survey. The independent variable is time (pre or post); the dependent variable is the scores on a test. Our research question is: Is the mean for the pre-study survey significantly different from the post-study survey's mean? Our null hypothesis is there will be no difference between the two times. Let us do an example together, open SPSS, and enter the following data for your samples.

Under Variable view (see tab at bottom of SPSS page), It should look like:

Name	Type	Width	Decimals	Label	Values	Ignore the rest
prescore	numeric	8	0	Prestudy score	None	Ignore the rest
postscore	numeric	8	0	Poststudy score	None	Ignore the rest

Go back to Data View and enter the following:

prescore	postscore
5	9
8	11
4	5
7	10
2	6
6	9
9	15
1	6
3	8
8	13

Go to *Analyze/ Compare Means/ paired samples t-test*. Move both of your score variables into Paired Variables. Press *ok*.

Your results should look like the following:

Paired Samples Statistics

		Mean	N	Std. Deviation	Std. Error Mean
Pair 1	prestudy score	5.30	10	2.751	.870
	poststudy score	9.20	10	3.190	1.009

Paired Samples Test

	Paired Differences					t	df	Sig. (2-tailed)
	Mean	Std. Deviation	Std. Error Mean	95% Confidence Interval of the Difference				
				Lower	Upper			
prestudy score poststudy score	-3.9	1.449	.458	-4.937	-2.863	-8.51	9	.000

What does this mean? Your two test times are significantly different from each other. So let us write it up as you would in your paper:

A paired sample t-test was conducted comparing the pretest survey (*M* = 5.3; SD = 2.75) to the posttest survey (*M* = 9.2; SD = 3.19). The result (*t*(9) = -8.51, *p*= .0001) indicates there is a significant difference between the test times and the null hypothesis is rejected.

What happens if the results were NOT significantly different, as in this example:

prescore	postscore
8	9
12	11
4	5
10	10
5	6
10	9
14	15
5	6
8	8
12	13

A paired sample t-test was conducted comparing the pretest survey (*M* = 8.8; SD = 3.39) to the experimental group (*M* = 9.2; SD = 3.19). The result (*t*(9) = -1.5, *p*= .168) indicates there is not a significant difference between the test times and the null hypothesis is retained.

Correlations

A correlation examines whether two variables are related. Remember a correlation tells you three things about the relationship: (a) *the direction of the relationship*. In a positive correlation as one variable increases the other increases. In a negative correlation, the two variables go in opposite directions, i.e., as one increases the other decreases. (b) *The form of the relationship*. The most common type of correlation is the Pearson correlation, which measures a linear (straight-line) relationship. However, there are other types of correlations (see a good statistics book). (c) *The degree of the relationship*. The Pearson correlation looks at how well the data fit a straight line. A perfect correlation, which is absolutely on the line, would be a 1.0. At the other extreme, data with no relationship would be a 0, and have no relationship to a straight line.

Let us do an example of a Pearson correlation together. An example might be the time to complete an exam and the person's grade on the exam. Our research question is: are the two variables related? Our null hypothesis is there will be no difference. So open SPSS and enter the following data for your sample.

Under Variable view (see tab at bottom of page), It should look like:

Name	Type	Width	Decimals	Label	Values	Ignore the rest
Examtime	numeric	8	0	Time to complete exam	None	Ignore the rest
Grade	numeric	8	0	Exam grade	None	Ignore the rest

Go back to Data View and enter the following:

Examtime	Grade
20	63
45	89
36	75
59	92
56	96
27	66
39	70
52	89
43	82
55	99

Go to *Analyze/ Correlate/ Bivariate*. Move both of your variables into *Variables*. Click *options* and include means and standard deviations. Press *Continue*. Make sure *Pearson, two-tailed*, and *Flag significant correlations* are checked. Press *ok*.

Your results should look like the following:

Descriptive Statistics

	Mean	Std. Deviation	N
Time to complete exam	43.20	12.925	10
Exam grade	82.10	12.879	10

Correlations

		Time to complete exam	Exam grade
Time to complete exam	Pearson Correlation	1	.943**
	Sig. (2-tailed)		.000
	N	10	10
Exam grade	Pearson Correlation	.943**	1
	Sig. (2-tailed)	.000	
	N	10	10

**. Correlation is significant at the 0.01 level (2-tailed).

To understand what is going on, we need to do a scatterplot. To do this, go to *Graphs /Chart Builder /Scatter/Dot*. Move the top left example to the box on top right. Move Time to complete on Y axis and Exam grade to X axis. Press *ok*.

It should look like this:

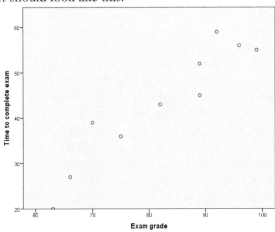

What does this mean? Time to complete the exam is significantly related to the exam grade. So let us write it up as you would in your paper:

A Pearson correlation was conducted comparing the time to complete the exam (M = 43.2; SD = 12.93) to the exam grade (M = 82.1; SD = 12.88). The result ($r(10)$ = .943, p= .0001) indicates there is a significant positive relationship between the two variables and the null hypothesis is rejected.

What happens if the results were NOT significantly different, as in this example?

Go back to Data View and enter the following:

Examtime	Grade
20	88
45	45
36	26
59	95
56	73
27	89
39	56
52	78
43	79
55	90

A Pearson correlation was conducted comparing the time to complete the exam (M = 43.2; SD = 12.93) to the exam grade (M = 71.9; SD = 22.57). The result ($r(10)$ = .131, p= .131) indicates there is not a significant relationship between the two variables and the null hypothesis is retained.

Independent Analysis of Variance (ANOVA)

An independent ANOVA examines whether the means of two or more separate samples are significantly different. An example might be a control group vs. a group with intervention A vs. a group with intervention B. The research question is: are the means for the three groups significantly different from each other? The independent variable is condition (control, group A or group B), the dependent variable is the scores on a test. The null hypothesis is there will be no difference between the groups. An important point: the ANOVA will only tell us if there is a significant difference present, it will NOT tell us, which groups are different from each other. To find this out, we will need to post hoc tests (more on this later). Let us do an example together. So open SPSS and enter the following data for your samples:

Under Variable view (see tab at bottom of page), It should look like:

Name	Type	Width	Decimals	Label	Values	Ignore the rest
Condition	numeric	8	0	Condition	*(see below)	Ignore the rest
score	numeric	8	0	Score	None	Ignore the rest

*For condition, labels: 1= control; 2 = group A, 3 = group B

Go back to Data View and enter the following:

Condition	Score
1	5
1	3
1	7
1	2
1	6
2	6
2	7
2	9
2	10
2	8
3	4
3	8

3	7
3	9
3	5

Go to *Analyze/ General Linear Model/ Univariate*. Move your score variable into *Dependent Variable*. Move condition into Fixed Factors. Go to *Post Hoc* (button on right side of variable screen), move condition into right box for post hoc tests. For now, choose Tukey's test (note, there are many different post hoc tests, check a stats book or the Pallant (2013) SPSS book to choose the correct one for your data). Press *continue* to return to the variable screen. Go to Options, move Overall and condition to right to display means. Also, check descriptive statistics. Press *continue* to return to the variable screen. Press ok.

Your results should look like the following:

Descriptive Statistics
Dependent Variable: Score

Condition	Mean	Std. Deviation	N
control	4.60	2.074	5
group A	8.00	1.581	5
group B	6.60	2.074	5
Total	6.40	2.293	15

Tests of Between-Subjects Effects

Dependent Variable: Score

Source	Type III Sum of Squares	df	Mean Square	F	Sig.
Corrected Model	29.200a	2	14.600	3.946	.048
Intercept	614.400	1	614.400	166.054	.000
condition	**29.200**	**2**	**14.600**	**3.946**	**.048**
Error	44.400	12	3.700		
Total	688.000	15			
Corrected Total	73.600	14			

a. R Squared = .397 (Adjusted R Squared = .296)

Multiple Comparisons

Dependent Variable: Score
Tukey HSD

(I) Condition	(J) Condition	Mean Difference (I-J)	Std. Error	Sig.	95% Confidence Interval	
					Lower Bound	Upper Bound
control	**group A**	-3.40*	1.217	**.040**	-6.65	-.15
	group B	-2.00	1.217	.266	-5.25	1.25
group A	control	3.40*	1.217	.040	.15	6.65
	group B	1.40	1.217	.503	-1.85	4.65
group B	control	2.00	1.217	.266	-1.25	5.25
	group A	-1.40	1.217	.503	-4.65	1.85

Based on observed means.
The error term is Mean Square(Error) = 3.700.
*. The mean difference is significant at the .05 level.

What does this mean? There is a significant difference between the three groups (see where I marked in **bold** above). This does not tell us which groups are different from each other, to find this out we did Tukey's post hoc tests and found the control varied significantly from group A (see data marked in **bold** above), no other groups differed. So let us write it up as you would in your paper:

An independent ANOVA was conducted comparing the control group (M = 4.6; SE = .86) to group A (M = 8.0; SE = .86) and group B (M = 6.6; SE = .86). The result ($F(2, 12)$ =3.95, p= .048) indicates there is a significant difference between the groups and the null hypothesis is rejected. Tukey's post hoc tests examined which groups differed. It was found that only the control group and group A differed (p< .05).

Repeated Measures ANOVA

A repeated measures ANOVA examines whether the sample means at different points in time are significantly different for the same group of people. An example might be a pretest, immediate posttest, and a posttest 6 mon. later. The research question is: are the means for the three times significantly different from each other? The independent variable is time (pretest, immediate posttest, 6 mon. posttest); the dependent variable is the scores on a test. The null hypothesis is there will be no difference between the time periods. An important point: the ANOVA will only tell us if there is a significant difference present, it will NOT tell us, which groups are different from each other. To find this out, we will need to post hoc tests (more on this later). Let us do an example together. So open SPSS and enter the following data for your samples:

Under Variable view (see tab at bottom of page), It should look like:

Name	Type	Width	Decimals	Label	Values	Ignore the rest
prettest	numeric	8	0	Pretest	None	Ignore the rest
posttest1	numeric	8	0	Immediate Posttest	None	
posttest2	numeric	8	0	6mon Posttest	None	Ignore the rest

Go back to Data View and enter the following:

Pretest	Immediate Posttest	6mon Posttest
3	6	9
5	8	3
2	5	5
4	9	7
1	6	4

Go to *Analyze/ General Linear Model/ Repeated Measures*. For the first screen (Within Subject Factor) write in Time where says *Factor 1*, give it 3 levels. Press *Define*. Move all of your variables into *Within Subjects Variables* box. Press *Options* and the *Descriptive statistics* and *Estimates of effect size* boxes in the area labeled *display*. Request post hoc tests by selecting Time in the *Factor and Factor Interactions* sections and moving it to the *Display Means* box. Check *compare main effects*. In the *Confidence interval adjustment* section, click on the down arrow and choose the option *Bonferroni*. Press *continue* and *ok*.

You will get a lot of tables for this; we are only going to use the following:

Descriptive Statistics

	Mean	Std. Deviation	N
Pretest	3.00	1.581	5
Immediate Posttest	6.80	1.643	5
6mon Posttest	5.60	2.408	5

Multivariate Tests[a]

Effect	Value	F	Hypothesis df	Error df	Sig.	Partial Eta Squared

	Pillai's Trace	.939	22.971[b]	2.000	3.000	.015	.939
	Wilks' Lambda	**.061**	**22.971[b]**	**2.000**	**3.000**	**.015**	**.939**
time	Hotelling's Trace	15.314	22.971[b]	2.000	3.000	.015	.939
	Roy's Largest Root	15.314	22.971[b]	2.000	3.000	.015	.939

a. Design: Within Subjects Design: time
b. Exact statistic

Pairwise Comparisons

Measure: MEASURE_1

(I) time	(J) time	Mean Difference (I-J)	Std. Error	Sig.[b]	95% Confidence Interval for Difference[b]	
					Lower Bound	Upper Bound
1	2	-3.800[*]	.490	**.004**	-5.740	-1.860
	3	-2.600	1.288	.341	-7.703	2.503
2	1	3.800[*]	.490	.004	1.860	5.740
	3	1.200	1.319	1.000	-4.025	6.425
3	1	2.600	1.288	.341	-2.503	7.703
	2	-1.200	1.319	1.000	-6.425	4.025

Based on estimated marginal means
*. The mean difference is significant at the .05 level.
b. Adjustment for multiple comparisons: Bonferroni.

What does this mean? There is a significant difference between the three times (see where I marked in bold above). This does not tell you which groups are different from each other, to find this out we did Bonferroni post hoc tests and found the pretest varied significantly from the immediate posttest (see data marked in bold above) no other groups differed. So let us write it up as you would in your paper:

A repeated measures ANOVA was conducted to compare scores at the pretest ($M = 3.0$; SD = 1.58), immediate posttest ($M = 6.8$; SD = 1.6), and the 6 mon. posttest ($M = 5.6$; SE = 2.4). The results (Wilks' Lambda = .061. $F(2, 3) = 22.97$, $p= .015$, multivariate eta squared = .939 [large effect]) indicates there is a significant difference between the time periods and the null hypothesis is rejected. Bonferroni post hoc tests examined which groups differed. It was found that only the pretest and immediate posttest scores differed ($p< .05$).

Regression

Multiple regression is a more sophisticated extension of correlation and is used when you want to explore the predicative ability of a set of independent variables (IV) on one continuous dependent measure (DV). There are different types of multiple regressions that allow you to compare the predictive ability of particular independent variables and find the best set of variables to predict a dependent variable. I will be looking at a standard multiple regression.

An example might be the time to complete an exam (IV1), the person's grade on the exam (IV2), and perceived stress (DV). The research questions are: 1) How well do time on the exam and grade on exam predict perceived stress? How much variance in perceived stress scores can explained by scores on these two IVs? 2) Which is the best predictor of perceived stress: time or grade?

Let us do an example of a multiple regression together. So open SPSS, first go to *Edit* on the menu, select *Options* and make sure there is a check in the box *No scientific notation for small numbers in tables*. Enter the following data for your sample. Under *Variable view* (see tab at bottom of page), it should look like:

Name	Type	Width	Decimals	Label	Values	Ignore the rest
Examtime	numeric	8	0	Time to complete exam	None	Ignore the rest
Grade	numeric	8	0	Exam grade	None	Ignore the rest
Stress	numeric	8	0	Perceived stress	None	Ignore the rest

Go back to *Data View* and enter the following:

Examtime	Grade	Stress
20	63	85
45	89	65
36	75	82
59	92	45
56	96	50
27	66	90
39	70	77
52	89	70
43	82	85
55	99	47

Go to *Analyze/ Regression/Linear*. Move your continuous DV (stress) into the *Dependent* box.

Move your IVs (exam time and grade) into the *Independent* box

For *Method*, make sure *Enter* is selected.

Click on the *Statistics* button

Select the following: *Estimates, Confidence Intervals, Descriptives, Model fit, Part and partial correlations,* and *Collinearity diagnostics*

In the *Residuals* section, select *Casewise diagnostics* and *Outliers outside 3 standard deviations*. Click on *Continue.*

Click on the *Plots* button

Click on **ZRESID* and move to the *Y* box

Click on **ZPRED* and move to the *X* box

In the section labeled *Standardized Residual Plots*, pick the *normal probability plot* option. Click on *Continue*

Click on the *Save* button

In the section labeled Distances, select *Mahalanobis* box and *Cook's*

Click on *Continue* and then *OK*

Now we will look at the output and interpretation. Your results should look like the following:

Descriptive Statistics

	Mean	Std. Deviation	N
perceived stress	69.60	17.063	10
Time to complete exam	43.20	12.925	10
exam grade	82.10	12.879	10

Model Summary

Model	R	R Square	Adjusted R Square	Std. Error of the Estimate
1	.884[a]	.781	.718	9.056

a. Predictors: (Constant), exam grade, Time to complete exam
b. Dependent Variable: perceived stress

ANOVA

Model	Sum of Squares	df	Mean Square	F	Sig.
Regression	2046.264	2	1023.132	12.474	**.005**
Residual	574.136	7	82.019		
Total	2620.400	9			

a. Dependent Variable: stress
b. Predictors: (Constant), grade, examtime

Correlations

		Perceived Stress	Time to complete exam	Exam Grade
Pearson Correlation	Perceived Stress	1.000	-.868	-.874
	Time to complete exam	-.868	1.000	.943
	Exam Grade	-.874	.943	1.000
Sig. (1-tailed)	Perceived Stress	.	.001	.000
	Time to complete exam	.001	.	.000
	Exam Grade	.000	.000	.
N	Perceived Stress	10	10	10
	Time to complete exam	10	10	10
	Exam Grade	10	10	10

ANOVA
(Reformatted to fit to page)

	Unstandardized Coefficients		Standardized Coefficient		
Model	B	Std. Error	Beta	t	Sig.
(Constant)	146.784	31.053		4.727	.002
Time to complete exam	-.518	.702	**-.393**	-.739	.484
exam grade	-.667	.704	**-.504**	-.948	.375

	95% Confidence		Correlations		Collinearity

	Interval for B					Statistics	
Model	Lower Bound	Upper Bound	Zero order	Partial	Part	Tolerance	VIF
(Constant)	73.354	220.214					
Time to complete exam	-2.177	1.141	-.868	-.269	-.131	.111	9.025
exam grade	-2.332	.998	-.874	-.337	-.168	.111	9.025

There are many aspects that can be checked, based on the analyses we have run; please see Pallant (2013) for an in-depth discussion of them.

Let us evaluate our model. Look in the Model Summary box and check the value under the heading R Square. This tells you how much of the variance in the DV (stress) is explained by the model (which includes the IVs exam time and grades). In this case, the value is .781 (see **bold**), so we can say the model explains 78.1% of the variance in perceived stress. We had a very small sample, however, so it is best to use the adjusted R square .718 or 71.8%, which is a better estimate. To assess the statistical significance of the result, we need to look at the table labeled ANOVA. This tests the null hypothesis that multiple R in the population equals 0. In our example, the model reaches statistical significance of .005 (see **bold**).

Next, take a look at the table of Coefficients and the column labeled Beta. Ignoring any negative signs we can see that exam grade made the largest contribution (.504) to explaining the DV, when the variance explained by all other variables are controlled. The Beta value for exam time was slightly lower (.393) indicating it made less of a contribution (see **bold**).

The results of the analyses allow us to the answer the two questions we posed at the beginning. The model, which includes the time to complete the exam and grade, explains 71.8% of the variance in perceived stress. Of these two variables, exam grade makes the largest contribution (beta = -.504), although exam time also made a statistically significant contribution (beta = -.393).

Covariates, Mediators, and Moderators

These are confusing and complex statistical terms; one way to think of them is as "third" variables. Research questions that ask how, when, for whom, which, and under what conditions require attention to additional ("third") variables that can explain how two variables are related. Mediation and moderation are two examples of this detailed examination of relations between variables (Kraemer, Kiernan, Essex, & Kupfer, 2008). There has been a great deal of interest in third variable analyses because they offer the potential to provide a more sophisticated understanding of interdependencies.

Mediation is defined as a relationship such that an independent variable causes a mediating variable, which then causes a dependent variable (MacKinnon, 2008). For mediation to exist, the following conditions must be met. First, there must be a substantial relationship between an independent variable and the mediating variable, and there must be a relationship between the mediating variable and the dependent variable when accounting for the independent variable.

Second, by definition, mediation requires a causal precedence such that the independent variable precedes and is a cause of the mediator, and the mediator must precede and be a cause of the dependent variable. Ideally, repeated measures of the mediator and dependent variable are available to investigate temporal relations, but often these causal relations must be inferred based on theory or prior research.

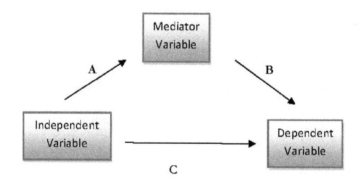

As an example, Barrera, Strycker, MacKinnon, and Toobert (2008) use analyses of mediation to evaluate the mechanisms by which the Mediterranean Lifestyle Program facilitates lifestyle modifications for patients with diabetes. Their approach evaluates if the intervention is successful in bringing about change in social-ecological resources (hypothesized mediators), and if increased social-ecological resources then predict improved health behaviors. Such an approach facilitates refinement of the program by building on successful components and either modifying or minimizing components that appear less effective in bringing about the desired effects.

In contrast, an examination of moderating factors considers the unique conditions under which two variables are related. A moderator

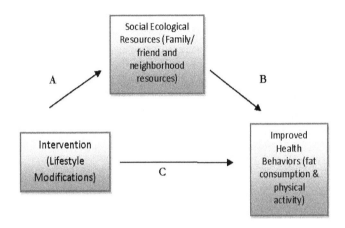

variable is one in which the relation between the independent variable and dependent variable changes across levels of the moderator. Although often confused with mediation, a moderator is not intermediate in the causal sequence from the IV to the DV. Moderators are included in statistical models as an interaction term. For the assessment of moderation effects, the relation between the independent and dependent variable must be different at different levels of a third variable. When the third variable is a grouping variable, then the relation between the independent and dependent variable is simply different between the two groups, for example, if the relation differs for males and females.

Analyses of moderation are useful for asking questions such as "When is stress dangerous to one's health?"; "Under what conditions are hostile people at greatest risk?" and "For whom is this intervention effective?" In analysis of variance (ANOVA) terms, a moderator effect can be represented as an interaction between an independent variable and a factor that specifies the appropriate conditions for its operation, that is, the effect of the independent variable depends upon the value of the moderator variable

An example is a study examining two different methods of teaching math. If students with strong reading skills do better on a math test with one method and those with low reading skills do better with the other, then reading skill level is functioning as a moderator variable.

	Method 1	Method 2
Hi reading skills	20	50

Low reading skills	40	30

One other type of third variable is a covariate, which has a relation with one or both of the independent and dependent variables, but does not appreciably change the relation between an independent and dependent variable when included in a statistical analysis. Covariates are generally not of theoretical interest, but are often included in a model to explain additional variability in a dependent variable. For example, Vella et al. (2008) include a number of covariates, including posture, caffeine intake, and body mass index, in their analyses of the influence of hostility and social interactions on ambulatory blood pressure. In the next chapter, I will examine analytic strategies for qualitative and mixed method studies.

CHAPTER 14
ANALYTIC STRATEGIES: QUALITATIVE AND MIXED METHOD

You have completed your interviews and maintained your field notes, the next step is to do the transcriptions. If you can do the transcriptions as you go, it is even better! You should include every utterance of the interviewee, including umms, laughter, etc. Incorporate your field notes and observations into the transcription (e.g., subject head down, begins to cry). The transcription is the most time consuming aspect, in my opinion.

You now have a ton of information from all of your interviews, what do you do with it? First, I suggest reading through all of your interviews several times. Think about them as you read them, what are the people saying? What are they NOT saying? Sometimes, what they avoid discussing is as interesting as what they do say. Try to put yourself in their place; you want to understand what their life is like.

Once you have a good feel for the data, the next step is to begin the analysis. There are a number of software programs available, such as Nvivo and Qualrus, but I am going to recommend a low-tech method I generally use. In this method, a matrix or table is used in Word. Picture a table as shown below for each interview question. Each person's response is copied into the table. You then carefully read each response and develop the coding for each one. As you do this, questions to ask yourself: What are the key points that are mentioned? What are the underlying emotions associated with the response? You will want to go through this process several times. The first time, use the participants' words in the codes. Then go through again and think about larger concepts that are present in different people's responses, can you find an overarching code in this data?

Subject #	What is your earliest memory?	coding
101	I remember my grandmother being sick, she had cancer. She passed away. I remember crying. It was summer time. I remember seeing her in her bed, not moving, with her eyes closed. I was with my mom.	
102	I remember my grandmother holding me in her arms with a polka dot cap. I remember her holding me in her arms, rocking me, trying to get me to go to sleep. The look in her eyes of happiness and content, of having me there as she rocked me to sleep with her polka dot night cap. I remember vaguely maybe the TV being on, maybe the news. I remember an air conditioner in the wall going.	
103	I was sitting at a table eating a sandwich and my mom was singing a song to me. It was a song I enjoyed her singing to me – I enjoyed the song and it made me feel comforted. I was focused on my mom's voice and hearing the story in the song.	

What coding would you give for each of the examples above? Try it and then see if yours are similar to mine (at the end of this section). It is always a good idea to have someone else independently code the responses and compare yours to theirs. For any you differ on, try to reach a compromise. You might think about if you know anyone who is at similar place in his or her dissertation process and would be willing to trade coding checks. If not, check with your committee member(s), perhaps they know another student who might work.

Once the coding is complete, the next step is to look for similarities across your interviews based up on the coding; these similarities are called themes. Were there any themes in the examples presented above (of course your data will have more people, three people do not make up a theme)? I have listed two possible ones at the end of this post.

Once themes are determined, the next step is to begin writing up Chapter 4, data analysis. You will want to give your themes and provide examples of quotes illustrating them.

My coding and themes
101- grandmother, death, visual imagery, with mother, crying (negative emotion)
102- grandmother, visual imagery, auditory, empathy (recognizing other's emotions)
103- mom, eating, auditory imagery, feelings of comfort

Possible Themes: female relative, visual and auditory imagery
Analyses: Mixed Method
By definition, a mixed method incorporates both quantitative and qualitative methods. There are several ways to analyze the data; I am going to discuss two. In the first method, the quantitative data is analyzed and the qualitative simply adds to an understanding of the data through quotes.

In the second method, the data are analyzed together. Typically, the quantitative data is analyzed first, using more sophisticated analyses, such as multiple regression. Then the qualitative data is transformed into quantitative data (see Creswell & Plano Clark, 2011). To do this you will need to develop a scoring rubric for the qualitative themes and codes you want to incorporate. Let us use the qualitative data from the previous section, in which we had three sample responses. I developed coding as follows:

101- grandmother, death, visual imagery, with mother, crying (negative emotion)
102- grandmother, visual imagery, auditory, empathy (recognizing other's emotions)
103- mom, eating, auditory imagery, feelings of comfort

I need to decide what is important to include in my data analysis (this will be related to your research questions). I decide I want to include any person mentioned; if a female relative, it will be designated as 1, a male relative will be 2, nonrelative female 3, etc. I am also interested in the use of imagery; if they mention visual images it will be 1, no visual will be 0. Auditory imagery will be 1, no auditory will be 0. Emotions in the self will be 1, and emotions mentioned in others will be 2. I would then enter this into SPSS along with the participants' scores on the quantitative measures that were used. The resulting SPSS entry would look something like this:

Subject#	Survey1 Total	Survey2 Total	Person	Visual Imagery	Auditory Imagery	Emotions
101	56	24	1	1	0	1
102	32	23	1	1	1	2
103	86	26	1	0	0	1

Then I will analyze the data using correlations and chi square to see if the scores on the surveys are related to the memories the participants reported. Presumably, I would have some theoretical rationale for doing this. If you would like to see what a mixed method analysis looks like in a journal, please see: Stadtlander et al. (2013). In the next chapter, we will begin writing Chapter 4 of your dissertation.

CHAPTER 15
DISSERTATION CHAPTER 4: DATA ANALYSES

You have collected and analyzed your data, so it is time to start writing Chapter 4 Analyses. You begin this chapter with briefly summarizing your study, restating your research questions, and a brief statement as why these questions are important. Then do a preview of Chapter 4 and what you will discuss.

If you have done a pilot study (which I always recommend), you need to provide details on it. So begin this section with a description of the pilot study and how it was done. Describe how you selected your pilot subjects, any important characteristics of them, and your procedure. Explain the purpose of your pilot study; you may have simply wanted to practice interviewing people or wanted to check how long the study takes. Alternatively, it may be done to confirm that your participants understand the questions you are asking and they may have other suggestions that affect your procedures. If you changed any procedures report it, describe why you felt it was necessary, and that you filed a change of procedure with the IRB.

The next section is the Settings section of the chapter. Here you would describe any personal or organizational conditions, which may have occurred since the study was approved. Some examples might be if you recruited people to talk about a particular social service program and that program's budget was cut in the midst of your data collection, it would be important for the reader to know this. Alternatively, perhaps you were in a car accident half way through your interviews, changing your appearance. It would again be important for the reader to be aware of such a change.

Demographics and Data Collection

First, you need to discuss the relevant demographic characteristics of your participants. Typical items include gender, race, and age, as well as any characteristics specific to your study. For example, if you interviewed homeless teen mothers, it would be important to know how long they have been on their own, their age, and the age of their children.

For all methods, the next section is Data Collection. You need to describe when the study was done (for example, months and year). Describe how you recruited your participants, and how many participated in all phases of the study. If you had to change any of your data collection procedures from what was listed in Chapter 3, indicate how and why it was changed (and that you went through the IRB to do so).

For Qualitative and Mixed Methods Studies. Describe the location of your study, how often you met with participants and the length of time both for individual interviews/surveys and for the total study. Next, describe how you recorded your interviews and how they were transcribed. If you encountered any unusual circumstances during your data collection describe it and how it affected your data collection (e.g., equipment failure, a participant died between interviews, etc.).

For Quantitative Studies. Describe your demographics as discussed above. Describe how representative your sample is to the population of interest or how proportional it is to the larger population if non-probability sampling is used (external validity). Provide results of basic univariate analyses that justify inclusion of covariates in your model, if applicable. For this section, keep in mind your reader should have a good picture of how you did your study, and would be able to replicate it based upon your description.

Data Analyses: Quantitative

Start by reporting descriptive statistics that appropriately characterize the sample. What does this mean? Look at frequencies for your demographics, such as gender, marital status, etc. For continuous variables (not in categories) you will need to compute the means and standard deviations or standard errors (check with your committee as to which they prefer). An example of such a continuous variable is age, the convention is to give these statistics like this (M = 43 yr., SD = 5.2). You will also discuss any total scores or sub-scores you may have calculated and their distribution.

The next step is to discuss and evaluate statistical assumptions as appropriate to the study. All statistical tests have specific assumptions, which must be considered (see Pallant, 2013, for an in-depth discussion of them). Let us take as an example, the assumptions for parametric tests (e.g., t-tests, analysis of variance) are: using an interval or ratio scale of measurement, random sampling, independence of observations (no measurement is influenced by another), a normal distribution, and homogeneity of variance (samples have similar variances). There are techniques to check these assumptions, and you would discuss in this section which ones you used and the results.

Next, you report your findings, organized by research questions and/or hypotheses. Include the exact statistics and associated probability values (some examples: $t(32)=3.1$, $p < .01$; $r(N=45)= .16$, $p > .05$). A reminder, if the probability is $< .05$ (less than), it is considered significant; if it is $> .05$ (greater than) it is not significant. You should include confidence intervals around the statistics, as appropriate (check with your committee). Include effect sizes, as appropriate (e.g., R^2, check with your committee as to what they prefer).

If you had multiple conditions, you may need to do post-hoc tests. Report the type and results of post-hoc analyses. You may have additional statistical tests of hypotheses that emerged from the analysis of main hypotheses and you will need to report those.

Finally, you may wish to clarify your results with tables and figures, include those as specified in the APA manual. There is very specific formatting for these, so check it out in the manual.

Data Analyses: Qualitative and Mixed Methods

This section asks you to describe how you went about analyzing your qualitative data. To begin, you will outline the overall process you used to move inductively from coded units to larger representations including categories and themes. If you followed a specific author's methods (e.g., Creswell) cite him or her.

Next, you move into the specifics of your data by describing the specific codes, categories, and themes that emerged from the data using quotations from your participants as needed to emphasize their importance. Keep in mind you are walking the reader through the process of your data analysis, so share specifics, how did you make decisions as to what were themes?

Finally, in most studies you will have a person or two who discussed experiences or ideas that were outside the normal experience of the others in your sample, these are called discrepant cases. Describe how these discrepant cases differed from the rest of the sample and how they were factored into the analysis. You should also consider whether there are obvious reasons for their differences, are these individuals older, younger, or in some other way different from others in the sample?

Evidence of Trustworthiness: Qualitative and Mixed Methods

An important element of qualitative studies is trustworthiness. In this section of Chapter 4, you will describe how you went about implementing the strategies and plans you laid out in Chapter 3. Let us review the commonly used methods that were mentioned earlier.

Credibility, which is comparable to internal validity. This is getting at the credibility of your data, common methods used are triangulation, prolonged contact, member checks, and saturation. You want to show your data are as accurate as possible.

Transferability, which is comparable to external validity. This is getting at the generalizability of your data to other groups. Common methods used are thick description and a variation in participant selection.

Dependability, comparable to reliability. You want to show the accuracy of your data methods, common methods are audit trails and triangulation. Triangulation is accomplished by asking the same research questions of different study participants and by collecting data from different sources and by using different methods to answer those research questions. Member checks occur when the researcher asks participants to review both the data collected by the interviewer and the researchers' interpretation of the interview data.

Confirmability, comparable to objectivity. This is the degree to which the findings are the product of the focus of the study and not of the biases of the researcher. One way to do this is through an audit trail. An adequate trail (or records) should be left to enable an independent auditor (such as the IRB) to determine if the conclusions, interpretations, and recommendations can be traced to their sources and if they are supported by the inquiry.

As with the other chapters in your dissertation, Chapter 4 ends with a summary. This summary should be structured around your research questions. So list each question and summarize the answers you found in your study. You will then end with a transition to Chapter 5.

Chapter 4: Lucy

Your future reader, Lucy, has reached the heart of your dissertation, Chapter 4. This is where she finds out what actually happened in your study! First, you will give her a quick overview of the study and why you were doing it. Then you jump into any pilot studies you did. It is important to indicate any deviations you made to your original plan in Chapter 3. Carefully lay out how you went about recruiting your sample for the pilot study and any changes you made, based upon what happened in the pilot. Lucy needs to very clear about where you are as you begin the main study.

Next, describe the setting of your study, remember that Lucy needs to know exactly how you went about it, so be detailed. Describe your participants, so Lucy can clearly see how your participants might differ from hers. Now clearly and in detail, explain how you went about your procedures with your participants. Lucy should be able to replicate your study based upon your description. So talk about how and where you recruited, how and where the study took place, how long it took, etc.

Next, in Chapter 4 is the data analysis section, describe how you went about analyzing your data. Discuss each step and how you went about it. Lucy should be able to take your data set, analyze it exactly as you, and get the same results you did.

Now present your results, Lucy is very excited to see how your study came out, so give her a careful and logical explanation of everything you found and relate your findings back to your research questions. Finally, summarize the chapter and what you will cover in Chapter 5. In the next chapter, I will explore Chapter 5 of your dissertation and what should be included in it.

CHAPTER 16
DISSERTATION CHAPTER 5: SUMMARY

Chapter 5 is the final chapter of your dissertation, while the end is in sight the work is not yet done! The chapter begins with a summary of the purpose of your study and why it was conducted. Resist the temptation to simply copy from earlier sections! You now have a very different view of the study then you did before you started, so take some time to rethink why you did this specific study and summarize it. Next, you will summarize the findings from Chapter 4, again it should not simply be copied, reword it.

Take a moment and think through what your results mean in the context of the literature. What have you added that we did not know before? Even if your study did not work, we know things that we did not know before you did it, whatever you tried does not apparently work well.

Interpretation

Begin this section with a description of the ways in which your findings confirm, disconfirm, or extend knowledge in the discipline. You will need to do this by comparing your findings with what has been found in the peer-reviewed literature described in Chapter 2. Yes, you will have to go back to Chapter 2 and see what other studies reported, describe how yours are the same or different. This is not something that can be done in a paragraph or even a page. Discuss each of your themes/ findings and determine how they fit in the literature.

Next, you turn to your theories, analyze, and interpret your study's findings in the context of the theoretical and/or conceptual framework, as appropriate. This section needs to be in-depth, what did your theory predict? How do your findings relate to the predictions? Do we need to rethink the theory? How? What needs to be added? Just be very sure your interpretations do not exceed the data, findings, and scope. You can always mention areas that still need to be studied.

What do you do if your study did not work as expected? For example, you got non-significant results or your interviewees did not say what you expected them to. Discuss what was expected based upon the literature, and then speculate as to why your results may not have come out as expected. Did you have a small sample? Were your subjects from a different area or population than previous studies? Think about theoretical implications of your findings, what does it mean to the theory that things did not work as expected? Should we consider changes in the theory? What advice do you have for future researchers in this topic area?

Limitations

The limitations section asks you to consider your sample and its similarities and differences from the population. Unless you carefully sampled thousands of people, your sample will not be representative of the population, which is fine, you just need to understand how it differs. Consider racial and cultural differences between your sample and the general population. Other things to consider are that people who volunteer to be in a research study are probably different from those who do not volunteer, so that is a limitation to mention. Think carefully about your recruitment and research methods, how did you recruit? Who would not have been included? Did you use a computer survey? Then people without a computer would not have been excluded. Again, all of this fine, it is just part of research, but it is important to understand the study's limitations.

Keep in mind that all studies have limitations; it is just part of the process. Describe the limitations to generalizability and/or trustworthiness that arose from execution of the study. Resist the temptation to simply copy from Chapter 1, carefully think about who participated in your study and what that means in terms of generalizability. An example might be if you did your study in a rural area, it may not be generalizable to urban areas. Again, this is fine, but you need to recognize it.

Recommendations

The Recommendations section asks you to think through what the next research steps may be. Remember that science is based upon building upon others' research; this is your chance to influence the future! Describe recommendations for further research that are grounded in the strengths and limitations of the current study as well as the literature reviewed in Chapter 2. Think about your research methods, what alterations do you suggest for future researchers? What aspects still need to be studied? Are there changes in theory that you think need to be made? Your study is now part of the literature in the field, what areas are left to explore? Think of this section as a time capsule that you are leaving for future researchers and students; leave them with a good picture of what you see as needing additional study.

Implications

The implications section asks you to think about social implications and your work. How could future researchers, practitioners, or the public use your results? The biggest problem students have in this area is that they overstate the implications. Be realistic, your study is not going to change the world as we know it. You are just adding one little piece to the puzzle.

One difficult issue is when you have non-significant results; your study does not come out as hypothesized. This requires you to carefully rethink all of the assumptions and the thought process that led you to make the hypotheses that you did. Could there have been other factors involved that you missed earlier? Consider your sample; were they a good representation of your population? Perhaps, the results might have been different if you had a larger sample. Take a look again at your data, were any of the findings going in the right direction, but did not reach significance? This is evidence that a larger sample may have been needed.

Conclusions

The final section of your dissertation is the Conclusions. In the conclusion section, you need to wrap up the study by summarizing the key issues. You need to provide a strong "take home" message that captures the key essence of the study. What do you want people to remember about your study? These are your final words on your study, make them memorable, and clear!

Chapter 5 Issues

Chapter 5 is the final chapter and discussion of your dissertation. One question that students ask me is "can I introduce new literature in Chapter 5?" This is not a straightforward question in that any new literature should only be related to new topics that have arisen through the analyses of the data. I will use as an example, a recent study of mine (Stadtlander et al., 2013). We found that people over the age of 85 who had escorts (such as family members) when they visited their physician, tended to indicate they liked their physician more and considered them more kind than people who went alone. Assuming that this had not been previously discussed in the literature review, in Chapter 5 it would be appropriate to report any research related to this new finding.

You must also think through the implications of your results. Given that the findings are correct, what does this mean for the population? How could such findings be explained? Let us return to the example I gave earlier that people over 85 who had escorts when they visited their physician, tended to indicate they liked their physician more and considered them more kind than people who went alone. What are the implications of such a finding? Some that we suggested are: it may be that escorts encourage patients to change physicians if they do not approve of them. On the other hand, having someone else approve of the physician may cause a halo effect (Greenwald & Banaji, 1995), improving the oldest-olds' perception of the physician. An alternative, is those who like their physician may be more motivated to get treatment, and thus more likely to secure an escort. Are there further ideas that you have thought of?

Notice that the reference given (Greenwald & Banaji, 1995) was probably not discussed in the literature review. There would have been no reason to discuss halo effects previously.

Chapter 5: Lucy

Chapter 5 is where you bring everything together for your future reader, Lucy. In this chapter is your opportunity for Lucy to follow your logic in how you are interpreting your findings. Begin by summarizing the results for her, and then move into relating the results back to the literature that you reviewed in Chapter 2. Explain to Lucy how your results fit into the theory you used for your study, if the results do not match the predictions from the theory, speculate as to why you think that is the case.

Discuss your ideas for future research, this section is very important to Lucy, she may want to take one of your research ideas and use it for her own dissertation. Explain your recommendations in terms of previous studies, as well as your study, and what your recommendations would bring to the literature.

Finally, relate to Lucy your study's social implications. These ideas may lead her to suggest an applied study that will lead to further social change. Finally, talk to her directly and leave with her with your final message that captures what you feel are the most important elements of your study.

References and Appendixes

There are several final sections of your dissertation, these are also important to your future reader, graduate student Lucy. First, are the references, Lucy needs to see the literature you are citing, so she can read more about the theory and studies that you have shared with her. Remember, her study will be building off yours, she needs to follow your train of thought and logic; the best way for her to do that is to follow the path you took by reading the same literature.

Next, are the very important Appendixes, this is where you give Lucy the documents that you used in the study. Your consent form, ads that you may have posted, permissions you received, and any other relevant information is posted here for Lucy. With this information, she knows exactly what your participants saw and how they were thinking about your study.

I hope you have grasped in these discussions that your dissertation is a time capsule, in a sense, to future researchers. Leave them full documentation, and careful explanations of the path that you followed in your dissertation journey.

Final Steps

You have written all five chapters, your dissertation is probably between 100-200 pages, you have put in many hours of work, thought, and sweat into this document. So what is next? First, your chair must approve it, and then it goes to your committee member. Expect changes, these are just part of the process. Once both of your committee members are happy with it, it typically goes to a university representative who will read through the entire paper and probably want more changes. I strongly urge patience at this point. Again, as I have mentioned many times, each person is responsible for their small piece of this paper and will be held accountable for the quality of the final product. Rest assured that everyone wants you to be done with the best quality paper possible.

These final steps often are very stressful for students; they are often nearly at the end of a term and feel a great deal of pressure. Keep reminding yourself, it will happen… the end is in sight. Patience will keep you from sleepless nights.

Every institution has different policies, but at some point, your paper will go through a Form and Style review. In this review, an editor goes through your paper indicating what will need to be done to be compliant with the dissertation publishing company. Meanwhile, use this time to prepare your PowerPoint for your defense.

As soon as you get the Form and Style review back begin working on the changes. In advance of the defense, you will want to prepare a PowerPoint for your committee. You will typically be given 20-30 minutes to talk about your project, check with your committee as to the number of slides they recommend. It is better to have just an outline on the slides. Concentrate on the analyses and results with just enough from your proposal to put it into context. Check with your chair as to how he or she likes it done.

On the day of the defense, have your computer on with your paper available. It is also a good idea to have some water available. Your committee will greet you and try to put you at ease. A few reminders, this is not a confrontational situation. I know it is called a defense, but it is really just a chance for the committee to hear about the project one more time and celebrate that you have completed it. It is typically very collegial, with everyone trying to make it the best project possible. After your 20-minute talk, your committee will ask you questions. They are just trying to clarify any remaining issues, there may be some minor changes needed in your paper. Some very common questions that you may be asked at the end of the defense: what are your plans now? Are you planning to follow up on your results in the future? Will you attend graduation?

After the defense, finish all of your Form and Style changes. Any final changes that came out of your defense should be completed. There may be some additional administrative checking; often minor changes will need to be made. And then... you are done!

Service after the Ph.D.

Something I would like you to think about is that once you have your doctorate you will be in a position to make a difference in your community and profession through service. Like what? You could be on the Board of Directors for a nonprofit you like. These are typically unpaid positions, where you get to influence the direction the group will go in the future. You may also be asked to do fundraising, so check on that before you agree; know what is involved. Also, ask about "fiduciary responsibility" (being responsible for money problems) and if the board has some type of liability insurance for its members (they should!).

Another type of service is using your skills that you have learned in your doctoral program as a volunteer in a nonprofit. Here is an example that I am currently doing. My local no-kill animal shelter collects a great deal of information about each animal and its new adopted owner, but they have not done anything with the data. I am entering all of the data into SPSS and analyzing a year of it for them. They can then use the analyses to better understand their programs and make future changes. I am hoping to publish this data, so I discussed it with the nonprofit's administrators in advance and got IRB approval from my university. This way I have cleared any obstacles for future publication opportunities.

As a researcher and doctoral scholar, you will have opportunities to make a difference in your community. I hope that you will step up and create change on this local level! You may also want to consider being an officer/ member of the board of directors for state and national professional organizations. Use your expertise for things beyond your own advancement, help your profession and community.

Final Thoughts

My mentee, we have made it through your entire dissertation project together! I am so proud of your dedication and persistence. Celebrate this huge accomplishment! For the rest of your life you will be entitled to have those letters: Ph.D. after your name. Go into the world, mentee, and do good things!.

CHAPTER 17
NEXT STEPS

You have done it! You graduated and have a Ph.D. after your name... and now what? Let us consider some next steps.

PSDS
After the excitement of finishing dies down, you may find yourself developing what has recently been called "Post-Doctoral Stress Disorder" (PDSD). PSDS is the realization that you have to make plans for the rest of your life, and decide what you are going to do next. You may feel that you are at a crossroads, with some of the following questions:

- Should I pursue an academic career?
- If I do go into academics, should I do so online or teach at a brick and mortar institution?
- Should I pursue a post-doctoral fellowship?

Coping with these issues often leads to feelings of depression and immobilization. Writing your dissertation was concrete with a definable end product. The whole career thing may feel vague and overwhelming. Let us break it down and work through your options and some next steps.

An Academic Position
If you are interested in teaching and doing research, then applying for an academic position may be the logical next step. You need to know that getting an academic position is a numbers game, in that, you will need to apply for many jobs to get an interview and a serious chance at one. For example, when I was applying for my first job, I sent out over 150 letters of

interest, got 2 interviews, and was offered both jobs. It is not unusual for there to be 300+ applications for each position, so be persistent!

You will need a curriculum vitae, a statement of research interests, a statement of teaching philosophy, and a basic cover letter for your academic applications. Do some online searches for each of these items and put yours together. You will have some decisions to make, such as, are you (and your family) willing to move for a job? Do you have teaching experience? If not, look for a temporary adjunct position with the goal of getting teaching experience for a more stable position later. Are you interested in an in-person teaching position at a brick and mortar institution or would you prefer an online position?

There are now a number of websites with academic job listings. Here are a few, also check your professional organizations (such as the American Psychological Association):

- http://www.onlinefacultycareers.com/
- http://www.simplyhired.com/
- http://us.jobs/
- http://www.indeed.com/
- http://academicjobsonline.org/ajo
- http://www.wileyjobnetwork.com/
- http://jobs.psyccareers.com/jobs/
- OnlineTeachingJobs@yahoogroups.com

a Yahoo group for online teachers owned/moderated by the Babb Group

- The Chronicle of Higher Education: http://chronicle.com/section/Home/5 This publication not only provides interesting reports on current events impacting academics but also publishes job ads regularly though there is a fee for this subscription
- United States Learning Association: www.usdla.org (job board is: www.usdla.org/job-board/)
- www.geteducated.com
- www.higheredjobs.com
- Visit college web sites for their currently listed openings.

Post-Doctoral Fellowships

For individuals who would like to get some advanced training in research, an option is to look for a post-doctoral fellowship. These are paid positions that allow you to work with top researchers in your field and get the opportunity for more specialized training, the chance to be published, and great networking contacts.

The negatives are that they do not pay well compared to faculty positions; they are temporary, typically only for one or two years, so you may need to uproot your family. You can find information on these types of positions in your professional organizations websites.

Rewrite Your Dissertation into an Article!

Your work related to your dissertation is not done until it in the professional literature for others to read and follow up with in future research. Most academic positions will want to see that you have some publications, get started with this requirement by rewriting your dissertation.

I am the editor of Walden University's *Journal of Social, Behavioral, and Health Sciences*. One of the most common questions I receive, as a journal editor, is how do I make my dissertation into an article? I will discuss this issue and offer some suggestions on how to approach this difficult task.

Let's review a few basics of the differences between a dissertation and a published journal article. An article, based on your project will be much shorter than your original dissertation. While a dissertation is often between 100-200 pages, a manuscript for a journal article is rarely over 30 double-spaced pages. A dissertation must exhaustively review the literature, however, the literature in an article is provided to put the study into context; the key issue is to lead the reader to clearly see the need for your study and the gap you are addressing. Much of the information in a dissertation is repeated throughout the paper- it can be characterized more as a book, a journal article should be succinct and to the point. So a few issues we have identified: your article should only have enough literature to put it into context, information should not be repeated frequently, and it should be succinct. Remember the basis of a journal article is the APA manual, so use the format it describes. Do check the journal's website for any exceptions it might prefer over the APA manual.

The first step, I recommend, is to do an outline of the project in an article format. Typically, this will be the following:

Cover page (title, your name, affiliation, and author notes),

Abstract (check journal requirements- typically 200-250 words). Keywords

Body of paper

Title of paper

(1-2 pgs.) Introduce the need for the study (why should we care about the topic?)

(2-5 pgs.) Literature review discussing variables

Method

Participants
Materials
Procedure
Results
Discussion
References

Literature

Reducing your 50-75 pages of Chapter 2 to a few pages of literature review in an article is a very daunting prospect! I suggest beginning by thinking through your key concepts/ variables. What does your reader absolutely have to know about to understand your study? Then write these down as the beginning of an outline for your article. My guess is it will look something like this:

Intro
Theory
Variable 1
Variable 2
Gap in the literature

With your outline as a map, now take each section individually and think about what is the most important literature you need to include? You do not have to do an exhaustive review, but you do need to show you understand the literature. You may find it helpful to treat each section as a summary of your literature on the topic in c. 2. Remember, you should not have more than five pages or so of literature, so keep to the essentials. Do a first draft and let it set for a day or two, then go back and see if you can eliminate any nonessential sentences. Have someone else read it for coherence, does it make sense to him or her, and make an argument for your study? Be sure you end the literature review sections with a couple of sentences emphasizing the gap you are addressing and why your study is needed. Mentioning your research questions helps the reader know where you are going.

Methodology

We are now into Chapter 3 of your dissertation, this needs to be cut down to just a couple of pages for an article. It is helpful to go to the APA manual and read the section on methodology and look at their examples. You also might want to read a recent article with similar methodology to yours. When you are ready, start with an outline, which will look something like this:

Method
  Participants
  Materials
  Procedure

Remember, your method section must be in sufficient detail that someone else can replicate your study based on your description. Therefore, each section needs to be written in detail, however, note that there are fewer sections than in your dissertation; so some things will need to be included in a sentence or two, such as a brief mention of the approval by the IRB (give approval number).

Results

The results section of your article is taking Chapter 4 of your dissertation and reducing it to the essentials. I find it helps to discuss the results through your research questions. Your results should be unbiased and provide enough detail that others can interpret them. Do not hide ones that did not come out as expected. Indicate whether your data violate the assumptions of the statistics you used.

It generally makes the most sense to set it up based on your research questions, keep it concise and to the point. Do not include unnecessary figures and tables. A good rule of thumb is if you discuss the data in detail in the text, do not also include a figure, or table on it.

Quantitative Studies. Keep your reporting of results non-biased and assume your reader has a professional knowledge of statistics (so do not explain basic concepts or give citations for common procedures). Be sure to explain how you handled any missing data in the analyses, and the percentage that were missing.

Qualitative Studies. Report your findings in a nonbiased way; explain how you went about your analyses. Provide participant quotes to illustrate your themes. It is a good idea to assign pseudonyms to participants and briefly provide any relevant information after each quote (e.g., Rose, age 68). Discuss any discrepant cases, and how these were addressed.

Discussion

The final text section of your paper is the Discussion, similar to the dissertation's Chapter 5. In your discussion, you will evaluate, interpret the results, and draw conclusions about them. Emphasize the theoretical or practical consequences of your findings. Be very careful that you are not misinterpreting or misrepresenting your findings (e.g., "the results are clear that older adults..." Did you examine ALL older adults? No? Then do not overgeneralize).

Begin your discussion with a clear statement of support or nonsupport for original hypotheses (it can also be structured in term of your research questions). Relate the findings to the previous literature, how do your results fit in with others' work? Your interpretations should take into account sources of bias and threats to internal validity. Also, consider limitations or weakness or your study. Bring in the theoretical implications of the study; does it fit with previous theories- why or why not? If not, could the theory be modified to account for your findings? Finally, end with problems remain unsolved, and what future areas of research have you identified?

Rewriting and Polishing

Once you have a draft of your article, it is time to begin the rewriting and polishing phase. Everyone has to do it, including very experienced writers. Accept that rewriting is part of the process, and spend that extra time now to save you pain later.

Where to start? I suggest reading through the draft in full, make notes to yourself (I use track changes) and mark areas that are not complete, that may not be clear to someone reading it for the first time, or that need more support with citations. Then start at the beginning and read each sentence aloud, is there a way to make it clearer, more concise? Picture your grandmother who knows nothing about your topic reading it, would she understand that sentence? Have you explained any terms that might be considered jargon? Check for any pronouns (they, he, and she), is it clear who the pronouns are referring to? Check your plurals versus possessives (this makes me crazy when they are wrong): plurals (e.g. "girls") do not have an apostrophe, possessives do have an apostrophe (e.g., "the girl's bike;" "the girls' bikes").

Do you know a former English major? Someone who is a great writer? If so, ask them to read through your paper and offer suggestions. Check your results section's APA format. There are very specific ways that statistics should be written, check the APA Manual that you are doing it correctly. If you are including tables or figures, then PLEASE read the sections on these in the APA Manual, not only on how to do them but also when to use them. Remember, professional articles use very few tables and figures.

Print out your references, then go through the paper crossing off each time you have cited the reference. They should come out even. Double check if the citation has 3+ authors (e.g., Smith, Jones, & Johnson, 2015) then use et al. after the first citation (Smith et al., 2015).

Updating your literature

As you are working on rewriting your dissertation into an article for publication, be sure that you update your literature. Research moves quickly these days with the internet, and you want to make sure when your paper is published it has the most current thinking. Authors often forget to check on literature related to theory, which can get them into trouble, so do your homework!

REFERENCES

American Psychological Association (2010). *Publication Manual of the American Psychological Association*, 6th Ed. DC: APA.

Barrera, M., Strycker, L.A., MacKinnon, D.P., & Toobert, D.J. (2008). Social-ecological resources as mediators of two-year diet and physical activity outcomes in Type 2 Diabetes patients. *Health Psychology, 27*(2):S118–S125.

Charney, D. S. (2004). Psychobiological mechanisms of resilience and vulnerability: Implications for successful adaptation to extreme stress. *Focus, 2,* 368-391.

Christensen, A. J. & Johnson, J. A. (2002). Patient adherence with medical treatment regimens: An interactive approach. *Current Directions in Psychological Science, 11*(3), 94-97.

Christensen, A. J., Moran, P. J. & Ehlers, S. E. (1999). *Prediction of future dialysis regimen adherence: A longitudinal test of the patient by treatment interactive model.* Paper presented at the annual meeting of the Society of Behavioral Medicine. San Diego.

Christensen, A. J., Edwards, D. L., Moran, P. J., Burke, R., Lounsbury, P., & Gordon, E. I. (1999). Cognitive distortion and functional impairment in patients undergoing cardiac rehabilitation. *Cognitive Therapy and Research, 23*(2), 159-168.

Cooper, C., Flint-Taylor, J., & Pearn, M. (2013). *Building Resilience for Success: A resource for managers and organizations.* NY: Palgrave.

Coutu, D. L. (2003). How resistance works. In *Harvard Business Review on building personal and organizational resilience.* Boston: Harvard Business School Publishing Corporation.

Creswell, J. W. & Plano Clark, V.L. (2011). *Designing and conducting mixed methods research*, 3rd ed. Los Angeles: Sage.

Duhigg, D. (2014). *The Power of Habit: Why we do what we do in life and business.* Random House.

Gilbert, E. (2015). *Big Magic: Creative Living beyond Fear.* Penguin Group.

Geertz, C. (1973). *The Interpretation of Cultures.* NY: Basic Books.

Greenwald, A. & Banaji, M.R. (1995). Implicit Social Cognition: Attitudes, self-esteem, and stereotypes. *Psychological Review, 102*(1), 4-27.

Kraemer, H. C., Kiernan, M., Essex, M., & Kupfer, D. J. (2008). How and why criteria defining moderators and mediators differ between the Baron & Kenny and MacArthur approaches. *Health Psychology, 27*(2):S101–S108.

MacKinnon, D. P. (2008). *Introduction to statistical mediation analysis.* Mahwah, NJ: Erlbaum.

MacKinnon, D. P. & Luecken, L.J. (2008). How and for Whom? Mediation and Moderation in Health Psychology. *Health Psychology, 27*(2 Suppl),

S99.

Maddi, S. R. & Khoshada, D. M. (2005). *Resilience at work: How to succeed no matter what life throws at you.* MJF Books.

Myers, S. B., Sweeney, A. C., Popick, V., Wesley, K., Bordfeld, A., & Fingerhut, R. (2012). Self-care practices and perceived stress levels among psychology graduate students. *Training and Education in Professional Psychology, 6*(1), 55-66.

Osborn, J. W. (2013). *Best practices in data cleaning.* DC: Sage.

Osborn, J. W. (2000). Prediction in multiple regression. *Practical Assessment, Research, & Evaluation, 7*(2).

Pallant, J. (2013). *SPSS survival guide,* 5th ed. Berkshire England: McGraw Hill

Ravitch, S. M. & Riggan, J. M. (2011). *Reason & Rigor: How Conceptual Frameworks Guide Research.* Sage Publications.

Rudestram, J. E. & Newton, R. R. (2007). *Surviving your dissertation: A comprehensive guide to content and process,* 3rd edition. Sage.

Saltzman, J. (1993). *If You Can Talk, You Can Write.* Grand Central Publishing.

Seidman, I. (2012). *Interviewing as qualitative research, 4th Ed.* NY: Teacher's College Press.

Smith, T. W. (2006). Personality as risk and resilience in physical health. *Current Directions in Psychological Science, 15*(5), 227-231.

Stadtlander, L., Giles, M., Sickel, A., Brooks, E., Brown, C., Cormell, M., Ewing, L., Hart, D., Koons, D., Olson, C., Parker, P., Semenova, V., & Stoneking, S. (2013). Independent Living Oldest-Old and Their Primary Health Provider: A Mixed Method Examination of the Influence of Patient Personality Characteristics. *Journal of Applied Gerontology.* doi: 10.1177/0733464813482182

Vella, E. J., Kamarck, T. W., & Shiffman, S. (2008). Hostility moderates the effects of social support and intimacy on blood pressure in daily social interactions. *Health Psychology, 27*(2):S155–S162.

Vogt, W. P., Gardner, D. C., & Haeffele, L. M. (2012). *When to use what research design.* NY: The Guilford Press.

Wagnild, G. M & Young, H. (1990). Resilience among older women. *Journal of Nursing Scholarship, 22,* 252–255.

APPENDIX A
A DISSERTATION CALCULATOR

Below is my version of a dissertation calculator. This is based on Walden University's process, check your own institution's process, and fill in reasonable times for each step. This is a "best case scenario," there are many unknowns that cannot be predicted (you run into IRB trouble, have difficulty getting subjects, etc.). I have been conservative with faculty response times (allowing 2 weeks for each, I have built chair response times into the time for each chapter). If you have writing issues, personal issues, you have many revisions, etc. it will take you longer. My calculator will get you done in 2 years.

	Target Date	Completed Date
Complete a draft prospectus (allow 2 weeks; this is for chair recruitment)		
Find your chair (allow a month)		
Complete prospectus (allow a term); at the same time, find your committee member (allow a month)		
Prospectus approved by chair, committee member, and program director (allow 2-4 weeks)		
Complete Chapter 2 (allow 2 terms)		
Chapter 2 Approved by chair		
Complete Chapter 1 (allow 6 weeks)		
Chapter 1 approved by chair		
Complete Chapter 3 (allow 6 weeks)		
Chapter 3 approved by chair		
Proof full proposal, references, complete appendixes, table of contents (allow a month)		
Proposal approved by chair, committee member (allow a month)		

Proposal approved by University Research Reviewer (URR; allow 2-4 weeks)		
Oral Defense of Proposal		
IRB Approval (allow a month)		
Conduct study (allow 1 term)		
Complete data analysis and Chapter 4 (allow a term)		
Chapter 4 approved by chair		
Complete Chapter 5 (allow a month)		
Chapter 5 approved by chair		
Proof full dissertation, references, appendixes, table of contents (allow 2-4 weeks)		
Dissertation approved by chair, committee member (allow a month)		
Dissertation approved by University representative (allow 2-4 weeks)		
Form and Style review (allow 2 weeks)		
Oral Defense of Dissertation		
Final University representative approval (allow 2 weeks)		
Chief Academic Officer (CAO) approval of abstract (2 weeks)		
DONE!		

APPENDIX B
Example Prospectus Outline

(Please keep in mind that your institution may have a specific format they want you to use)

Patient Personality Characteristics and Physician Satisfaction
in the Oldest Old

I. Problem Statement
    A. Patient Satisfaction
    B. Relate to my study
II. Significance
    A. Oldest old
    B. Cost of health care
III. Background
    A. Physician–patient relationship
    B. Oldest old and physicians
    C. Variables
        1. Patient satisfaction
        2. Locus of Control
        3. Resilience
        4. Self-Efficacy
IV. Framework
    A. Patient-by-treatment-context interactive model
    B. Predictions
V. Research Question(s)
    A. How do the oldest describe their satisfaction with their physician relative to their reported health practices?
    B. How do scores on the self-efficacy measure interact with satisfaction with their physician relative to their reported health practices?
    C. How do scores on the resiliency measure interact with satisfaction with their physician relative to their reported health practices?
    D. How do scores on the LOC measure interact with satisfaction with their physician relative to their reported health practices?
VI. Nature of the Study
    A. Power analysis
    B. Recruitment
    C. Inclusion criteria

D. Measures
    1. Patient Satisfaction
    2. Locus of Control
    3. Resilience
    4. Self-Efficacy
VII. Possible Types and Sources of Information or Data
    A. Scores
    B. Analyses
IIX. References

APPENDIX C: Example Prospectus

Patient Personality Characteristics and Physician Satisfaction
in the Oldest Old
Mary E. Student

Patient Personality Characteristics and Physician Satisfaction
in the Oldest Old

Problem Statement

There is a large literature on general patient satisfaction (Hertz, 2012; Lee & Kasper, 1998; Sherbourne et al., 1992). Patient satisfaction is an indicator of quality of care; however, such studies do not tend to examine the relationship of patients' responses with their personality.

Kong, Camacho, Felman, Anderson, and Balrishnan (2007) reported those over 65 of age had higher physician satisfaction scores and were less concerned with waiting times than were the younger adults. Lee and Kasper (1998) found relative to 65-69 year olds, people 80-84 were 20-30% less likely to be highly satisfied with their quality of care and physician quality. The older patients objected to the physician's lack of technical skills and interpersonal manner. The sample was limited to people under the age of 85, not the oldest-old. In addition, medical schools have made a recent effort to train physicians in geriatric care (Croasdale, 2008; Siegler & Capello, 2005), which may affect the current elderly's opinions of their physician.

The present study will examine a sample of independently living oldest-old adults from across the United States using a quantitative method. This method will allow the opportunity to survey healthy oldest-old patients as to their satisfaction with their physicians. There is a lack of research examining certain oldest-olds' individual characteristics that are known to be associated with health care and health providers. Thus, the current study also examines the relationship between Locus of Control (LOC), resilience, and self-efficacy to participants' opinions of their physician.

Significance

The 2000 U.S. Census (2001) reported 4.2 million people were over the age of 85 (1.5% of the population), this group has been designated the "the oldest-old" by demographers, and is the most rapidly growing age group. Currently the cost of health service utilization for the oldest-old averages $22,000 per year compared to $9,000 for individuals 65-74 years old (Krause, 2010). It would be logical to assume individuals on the less healthy side of the spectrum, who require nursing care or are in facilities (21.9% of this age group, Gist & Hetzel, 2004), bias this $22,000 mean. However, little is known about the oldest-old who are on the healthy end of the continuum. How do these individuals interact with their physician and how do their personalities affect the interaction? This quantitative study will examine this question.

Background

The relationship between the physician and patient is unique; in a medical encounter, often involving the meeting of two strangers, the patient reveals very personal topics and an examination of the patient's body occurs (Adelman, Greene, & Ory, 2000). How physicians handle such encounters can mean the difference between a patient following suggested medical advice or disregarding it (Adelman et al., 2000).

Wolinsky, Mosely, and Coe (1986; Wolinsky, Arnold & Nallapati, 1988) reported the oldest-old in their sample had fewer physician visits than did younger individuals. Wolinsky et al. (1988) speculated the decline in physician visits might be due to a general decline in mobility, making accessing health care more difficult. This is a reasonable assumption for the least healthy individuals, but it is not clear if this assumption holds for the more healthy members of this age group.

Locus of Control (LOC)

LOC is derived from Rotter's (1966) social learning theory, Rotter hypothesized people who view reinforcements as contingent on their own behavior (internals) are better adjusted than those who see reinforcements as determined by fate, chance, or powerful others (externals). The three subscales within the LOC measure are internal control, powerful others, and chance (Levenson, 1973; Rotter, 1966).

Rennemark, Holst, Fagerstrom, and Halling (2009) found a negative correlation between physician visits and functional ability, education level and internal LOC. High scores on the powerful others and chance subscales are predictors of patients' trust in their physician (Brincks, Feaster, Burns, & Mitrani, 2010). High internal LOC scores also tend to be correlated with being proactive in seeking information, making health modifications, and treatment adherence (Macaden & Clarke, 2010).

Resilience

Resilience moderates the negative effects of stress and promotes adaptation (Wagnild, 2009; Wagnild & Young, 1993), and is described as an enduring personality characteristic (Foster, 1997). Nygren et al. (2005) suggested that the development of resilience constitutes a form of compensation for losses of functional capacity and physical health. Leppert, Gunzelmann, Schumacher, Strauss, and Brahler (2005) reported that higher scores on the resilience scale correlated with lower rates of subjective complaints, and has been associated with health-promoting behaviors (Wagnild, 2000). Higher resilience has been found to be correlated with higher self-efficacy (Caltabiano & Caltabiano, 2006); it has also been found to be correlated with LOC in women with traumatic experiences (Friedman, 2009), but this relationship has not been previously examined using the

Wagnild and Young scale in the oldest old.

Self-Efficacy

Self-efficacy is defined as people's beliefs in their own abilities to manage upcoming situations and unexpected events (Bandura, 1986; Bandura, Barbaranelli, Caprara, & Pastorelli, 1996). Bandura (1986, 1993) suggests self-efficacy beliefs regulate an individual's ability to deal with stress and anxiety when faced with unexpected and stressful events. Previous research has reported self-efficacy (Schwarzer & Jerusalem, 1995) correlates with LOC (Rotter, 1966). A recent study by Halisch and Geppert (2012) reported a similar finding in an elderly population; however, the percentage of oldest old in their sample was limited. The present study will confirm whether the finding is evident in the current oldest-old sample.

Clayman, Pandi, Bergeron, Cameron, Ross, and Wolf (2010) noted self-efficacy influences the older patient's ability to act on information disseminated during a physician visit, as well as, confidence in asking questions of the doctor. Individuals with higher self-efficacy are more likely to benefit from health education interventions (Kostka & Jachimowicz, 2010), as they are able to perceive and apply the important information. The present quantitative study will examine the interrelationships between LOC, resilience, self-efficacy, and opinions of the oldest-old about their physician.

Framework

The patient-by-treatment-context interactive model of Christensen and Johnson (2002) provides the framework for the study. The model proposes that the relationship between patient characteristics (e.g., personality and beliefs) and patient adherence (e.g., preventative care) is moderated by the treatment context (e.g., physician characteristics and behavior). The model has been successfully applied to specific illnesses; for example, renal insufficiency and hemodialysis (Christensen, Moran, & Ehlers, 1999) and cardiac rehabilitation (Christensen et al., 1999). It does not appear to have been previously applied in the present context of ongoing preventative care in older adults. The patient (LOC, resilience, self-efficacy) and treatment (physician characteristics) variables in the current study were derived from the literature and are consistent with this model.

Based upon the patient-by-treatment-context interactive model of Christensen and Johnson (2002), adherence (preventative care) is expected to be best when the patient's characteristics (personality) are consistent with the treatment context (physician characteristics and behavior; Christensen, 2004). Thus, in the current study, there should be consistent preventative care (adherence) when the patient has higher internal LOC (being proactive in health), higher resilience (inner strength and optimism, health-promoting behaviors) and higher self-efficacy (more likely to seek information and self-confidence) and to indicate that they are satisfied with their physician (treatment). In addition, it would be expected that there would be less preventative care (lack of adherence) when the patient has lower internal LOC (i.e., external; not proactive in health), higher powerful others and chance scores (increased trust in physician). Other expectations include lower resilience (higher level of subjective complaints, fewer health-promoting activities), and lower self-efficacy (less likely to apply health interventions [preventative care] and less self-confidence) and to indicate that they feel satisfied with their physician (treatment).

Research Question(s)

RQ1. How do the oldest describe their satisfaction with their physician relative to their reported health practices?

RQ2: How do scores on the self-efficacy measure interact with satisfaction with their physician relative to their reported health practices?

RQ3: How do scores on the resiliency measure interact with satisfaction with their physician relative to their reported health practices?

RQ4: How do scores on the LOC measure interact with satisfaction with their physician relative to their reported health practices?

Nature of the Study

A power analysis using G*Power indicated that for a correlation study ($\alpha = .05$, Beta = .95), 138 participants will be required. The participants will be recruited through area Agencies on Aging and community/ senior centers in a large metropolitan area. The surveys will be conducted individually in an environment comfortable to the participant.

A modified Mini Mental Status Exam (MMSE) to check cognitive status will be conducted. Other inclusion criteria include being able to read English and able to hear adequately for the instructions. All participants will complete a consent form; upon passing the MMSE they will complete the surveys. The study is expected to take about an hour. Participants will complete a detailed demographic survey and the following measures:

Patient Satisfaction. Johnson and Muir's (2013) patient satisfaction in the elderly scale will be used. This is a 10 item scale asking patients about their recent experience with their physician. An example question is "My physician understands aging related issues."

Locus of Control. The Levenson Multidimensional Locus of Control scale (Levenson, 1973) is a 24-item assessment measure, which includes three separate subscales: internal LOC, powerful-others LOC, and chance LOC. Respondents were required to indicate the extent to their agreement with statements on a six-point scale ranging from "strongly agree" to "strongly disagree." The internal scale statements include items such as, "When I make plans, I am almost certain to make them work." The powerful-others scale statements include items such as, "I feel like what happens in my life is mostly determined by powerful people." The chance scale statements include items such as, "When I get what I want, it is usually because I'm lucky."

Resilience. Wagnild and Young's (1990) resilience scale is comprised of 25 items reflecting five characteristics of resilience: inner strength, competence, optimism, flexibility, and the ability to cope effectively when faced with adversity. Respondents indicated the extent to which statements apply to them on a seven-point scale ranging from "disagree" to "agree". An example statement is: "When I make plans I follow through with them."

Self-Efficacy. The Generalized Self-Efficacy scale (Schwarzer & Jerusalem, 1995) is a 10-item scale that assesses the strength of an individual's belief in his or her own abilities to respond to unexpected and stressful situation. Respondents are required to indicate the extent to which statements apply to them on a four-point scale from "Not at all true" to "Exactly true". The statements include items such as, "I can always manage to solve difficult problems if I try hard enough." A total score is derived by summing the scores for all items, yielding a maximum score of 40. The higher the score the greater is the level of general self-efficacy.

Possible Types and Sources of Information or Data

The quantitative surveys will result in four scores. An initial correlational analysis will examine relationship between them. A linear regression will examine the impact of each survey on patient satisfaction.

References

Adelman, R. D., Greene, M.G., & Ory, M.G. (2000). Communication between older patients and their physicians. *Clinics in Geriatric Medicine, 16*(1), 1-24.

Bandura, A. (1986). *Social foundations of thought and action: A social cognitive theory.* Englewood Cliffs, NJ: Prentice Hall.

Bandura, A. (1993). Perceived self-efficacy in cognitive development and functioning. *Educational Psychologist, 28*, 117-148.

Bandura, A., Barbaranelli, C., Caprara, G., & Pastorelli, C. (1996). Multifaceted impact of self-efficacy beliefs on academic functioning. Child Development, 67(3), 1206-1222. doi:10.2307/1131888

Brincks, A., Feaster, D., Burns, M., & Mitrani, V. (2010). The influence of health locus of control on the patient-provider relationship. *Psychology, Health & Medicine, 15*(6), 720-728.

Caltabiano, M.L., & Caltabiano, N.J. (2006, November). *Resilience and health outcomes in the elderly.* Paper presented at the 39th national conference of the Australian Association of Gerontology, Sydney, New South Wales.

Christensen, A. J. & Johnson, J. A. (2002). Patient adherence with medical treatment regimens: An interactive approach. *Current Directions in Psychological Science, 11*(3), 94-97.

Clayman, M. L., Pandit, A. U., Bergeron, A. R., Cameron, K. A., Ross, E., & Wolf, M. S. (2010). Ask, understand, remember: A brief measure of patient communication self-efficacy within clinical encounters. *Journal of Health Communication: International Perspectives, 15*(Suppl. 2), 72-79.

Foster, J.R. (1997). Successful coping, adaptation, and resilience in the elderly: An interpretation of epidemiologic data. Psychiatric Quarterly, 68(3), 189-219.

Friedman, A. T. (2009). *Resiliency in women with early traumatic experiences: An examination of level of secure attachment, optimism, spiritual well-being, locus of control, psychological equilibrium, and social support as potential predictors of successful outcomes.* New York University. ProQuest Dissertations and Theses, 134.

Gist, Y. J., & Hetzel, L. I. (2004). *We the people: Aging in the United States.* (US Census Bureau Publication No. CENSR-19). Washington, DC: U.S. Government Printing Office.

Halisch, F., & Geppert, U. (2012). Personality determinants of subjective well-being in old age: Cross-sectional and longitudinal analyses. *Motivation, Consciousness and Self-Regulation*, 139–171.

Kostka, T., & Jachimowicz, V. (2010). Relationship of quality of life to dispositional optimism, health locus of control and self-efficacy in older subjects living in different environments. *Quality of Life Research, 19*(3), 351-361.

Krause, N. (2010). Close companions at church, health, and health care use in late life. *Journal of Aging & Health, 22*(4), 434-453

Leppert, K., Gunzelmann, T., Schumacher, J., Strauss, B., & Brahler, E. (2005). Resilience as a protective personality characteristic in the elderly. *Psychotherapie, Psychosomatik, Medizinishe Psychologie, 55*(8), 365–369.

Levenson, H. (1973). Multidimensional locus of control in psychiatric patients. *Journal of Consulting and Clinical Psychology, 41*(3), 397-404.

Macaden, L., & Clarke, C. (2010). The influence of locus of control on risk perception in older South Asian people with Type 2 diabetes in the UK. *Journal of Nursing & Healthcare of Chronic Illnesses, 2*(2), 144-152.

Nygren, B., Aléx, L., Jonsén, E., Gustafson, Y., Norberg, A., & Lundman, B. (2005). Sense of coherence, purpose in life and self-transcendence in relation to perceived physical and mental health among the oldest old. *Aging and Mental Health, 9*(4), 354–362.

Rennemark, M., Holst, G., Fagerstrom, C., & Halling, A. (2009). Factors related to frequent usage of the primary healthcare services in old age: findings from the Swedish National Study on Aging and Care. *Health & Social Care in the Community, 17*(3), 304-311. doi:10.1111/j.1365-2524.2008.00829.x

Rotter, J. B. (1966). Generalized expectancies for internal versus external control of reinforcement. *Psychological Monographs: General and Applied, 80*, 1–28.

Schwarzer, R., & Jerusalem, M. (1995). Generalized Self-Efficacy scale. In J. Weinman, S. Wright, & M. Johnston, *Measures in health psychology: A user's portfolio. Causal and control beliefs* (pp. 3-37). Windsor, England: NFER-NELSON

U.S. Census (2001). *The 65 Years and Over Population: 2000.* Retrieved July 26, 2007 from http://www.census.gov/prod/2001pubs/c2kbr01-10.pdf

Wagnild, G. (2009). A review of the resilience scale. *Journal of Nursing Measurement, 17*(2), 105-113.

Wagnild, G. M. & Young, H.M. (1993). Development and psychometric evaluation of the Resilience Scale. *Journal of Nursing Measurement, 1*(2), 165-178.

Wagnild, G.M & Young, H. (1990). Resilience among older women. *Journal of Nursing Scholarship, 22*, 252–255.

Wolinsky, F.D., Arnold, C.L., & Nallapati, I.V. (1988). Explaining the declining rate of physician utilization among the oldest old. *Medical Care, 26*(6), 544-553.

Wolinsky, F.D., Mosely, R.R., & Coe, R.M. (1986). A cohort analysis of the use of health services by elderly Americans. *Journal of Health and Social Behavior, 27*, 209-219.

APPENDIX D
EXAMPLE CHAPTER 2 OUTLINE

I. Introduction

    A. Why study is important

    B. Gap in literature

II. Search Strategy

    A. Databases used

    B. Search Terms

III. Theories

    A. Theories of Successful Aging

        1. Activity Theory

        2. Disengagement Theory

    B. Patient-by-treatment-context interactive model (Christensen & Johnson, 2002)

IV. Concepts/ philosophy

    A. Info on mixed methods, philosophy behind it

V. Literature Review

    A. Aging and the elderly, include demographics

        1. Include methods used previously

        2. Previous findings

        3. What is missing from previous research?

        4. What does my study add?

    B. Elderly and health care, why do we care about topic?

        1. Include methods used previously

        2. Previous findings

        3. What is missing from previous research?

        4. What does my study add?

    C. Elderly and their health care provider

        1. Include methods used previously

2. Previous findings

3. What is missing from previous research?

4. What does my study add?

D. Survey instruments

1. Resilience

a. Used with my age group?

b. Used in health care research?

c. Used in health care providers research?

2. Locus of Control

a. Used with my age group?

b. Used in health care research?

c. Used in health care providers research

VI. Summary and Conclusions

ABOUT THE AUTHOR

Dr. Lee Stadtlander received her doctorate in Experimental Psychology from Ohio State University in 1993. Her research interests at that time were psycholinguistics, learning, memory, and aging. She then was a professor at Montana State University in Bozeman for 11 years (and still lives there). She then re-specialized in Clinical Health Psychology through Fielding University (this is a second doctorate). As part of her re-specialization, she completed a one-year internship at the Cross Cancer Institute in Edmonton Alberta, Canada. She retains an interest in counseling cancer patients and all things medically related. She began working for an online institution, Walden University, in 2005 and is now the Coordinator of the Doctoral Health Psychology program. She has been the Editor of Walden University's *Journal of Social, Behavioral, and Health Sciences*, since 2016. She received Walden University's highest faculty honor, the Presidential Award for Faculty Excellence, in 2017.

Dr. Stadtlander has mentored many doctoral students, and has had as of this printing, 30 doctoral students graduate whose dissertation committee she chaired. She encourages you to check out her Facebook page for this book and see the most current advice on the dissertation process: https://www.facebook.com/findingyourwaytoaphd. Please feel free to contact her and share your comments, successes, and concerns on Facebook or email her at: lstadtlander@gmail.com

CPSIA information can be obtained
at www.ICGtesting.com
Printed in the USA
LVHW050314010721
691578LV00014B/2297

9 781981 513987